M000268475

# Praise for
# Live WELLthy

"Dawn Dahlby calls on each of us to dig deep within and discover not just *how* we interact with our finances, but *why* we have the relationship with money that we do. *Live WELLthy* helped me get to the root of that question and has enabled me to live in abundance instead of scarcity."

—**LOREN LAHAV,** best-selling author, international speaker, and CEO of True

"*Live WELLthy* gives us permission to achieve balance in an unstable world. That right balance is different for everyone, but Dawn Dahlby gives you the tools to discover yours for yourself and know how to implement it in your life."

—**JOSH JALINSKI,** CEO of Jalinksy Advisory Group, host of *The Financial Quarterback* on 710 AM WOR

"Dawn Dahlby has lived a life of scarcity and abundance and she is the first to tell you that abundance is the way to go! In her blockbuster new book *Live WELLthy*, Dawn Dahbly provides you with a proven strategy for transforming your entire life--spiritually, emotionally, and financially--into a life you love. If you have been craving a life filled with love and abundance, *Live WELLthy* is a MUST read!!"

—**DR. PATTY ANN TUBLIN,** founder and CEO of Relationship Toolbox LLC

"We all work hard to build wealth, but Dawn Dahlby reminds us that our money should be working just as hard, if not harder, *for us.*"

—**DERRICK KINNEY,** author of *Wall Street Journal* and *USA Today* bestseller *Good Money Revolution*

Own Your **WORTH**
Grow Your **WEALTH**

# LIVE
# WELLthy

## DAWN DAHLBY

CFP®, BFA™, and CRPC®

GREENLEAF
BOOK GROUP PRESS

LIBRARY OF
CONGRESS
SURPLUS
DUPLICATE

2022911199

*Live WELLthy*™ is designed to provide accurate and authoritative information in regard to the subject matter covered. It is sold with the understanding that neither the author nor the publisher is offering or rendering legal, financial, accounting, or any other professional services by publishing this book. As each individual situation is unique, a personalized one-on-one assessment with a qualified professional should be sought for expert analysis and assistance, especially in areas that include financial planning, tax strategies, and investment management. The stories and examples in this book use hypothetical annual rates of return strictly for illustration purposes only.

Past results do not guarantee future performance. Additionally, performance data, in addition to laws and regulations with investments and taxes change over time, which could change the status of information in this book. This book is sold with the understanding that it is not intended as a recommendation to use any specific wealth advisor or to serve as a basis for any financial decisions.

No warranty is made with respect to the completeness or accuracy of the information contained in this book, and both the author and the publisher specifically disclaim any liability, loss, or risk, personal or otherwise, which is incurred as a consequence, directly or indirectly, of the use and application of any of the contents in this book.

Published by Greenleaf Book Group Press
Austin, Texas
www.gbgpress.com

Copyright © 2023 Dawn Dahlby CFP®, BFA™, and CRPC®

All rights reserved.

Thank you for purchasing an authorized edition of this book and for complying with copyright law. No part of this book may be reproduced, stored in a retrieval system, or transmitted by any means, electronic, mechanical, photocopying, recording, or otherwise, without written permission from the copyright holder.

Distributed by Greenleaf Book Group

For ordering information or special discounts for bulk purchases, please contact Greenleaf Book Group at PO Box 91869, Austin, TX 78709, 512.891.6100.

Design and composition by Greenleaf Book Group and Mimi Bark
Cover design by Greenleaf Book Group and Mimi Bark
Cover images used under license from ©Shutterstock.com/KanokpolTokumhnerd; ©Shutterstock.com/AlexVector
Think2Perform Values Exercise copyright held by and used with permission of Douglas A. Lennick ©2022

Publisher's Cataloging-in-Publication data is available.

Print ISBN: 979-8-88645-028-6

eBook ISBN: 979-8-88645-029-3

To offset the number of trees consumed in the printing of our books, Greenleaf donates a portion of the proceeds from each printing to the Arbor Day Foundation. Greenleaf Book Group has replaced over 50,000 trees since 2007.

Printed in the United States of America acid-free paper

23  24  25  26  27  28    10  9  8  7  6  5  4  3  2  1

First Edition

# Contents

## PART THREE: Grow It! Grow Your Financial Wealth and Your Life

# Preface

S ometimes we don't know what will end up being the catalyst to great change in our lives. My life was significantly altered one night in August 2018, two months after my husband and two teenage daughters and I moved across the country from Minnesota to Arizona. We were eager to embrace a new life that was more aligned with how we wanted to live—away from long, cold winters, for one thing. Since we were in an unfamiliar rental home, my daughter Olivia asked me to sleep with her on that stormy night as she was afraid of the booming thunder, piercing lightning, and pounding rain. Early the next morning I was jolted out of sleep by my husband's banging on the bedroom door. "Your mom," he said. His face looked pale and distraught. Clearly something was wrong.

Mom had just flown to Phoenix the previous day and was staying with us before moving into her new condo, after having decided to move from Wisconsin. Unable to speak, I rushed into the guest bedroom and found Mom slumped over in bed, face down. I tried desperately to wake her but quickly realized she was gone, gone on the very day we planned to move her into her new condo where she was going to start her new life close to us.

Fighting through an ocean of emotions and waves of tears, I had no idea what to do. So I started as I often do when I'm at a standstill: I start asking, "Why?" Over the next few days I dug deeply, did a lot of remembering, and a lot of research. To sum up what I found: my mom's heart gave out. Why? She had diabetes. She was addicted to alcohol. Why? She'd spent years trying to numb her pain—not her physical pain, but her emotional pain.

Why was she in such pain? Thinking back on my years of conversation with her, watching and sometimes challenging her repeated irrational, impulsive, sometimes desperate behaviors, I realized that my mom suffered all her life from her negative self-perceptions. She believed she had no worth and no wealth. These faulty beliefs, conflicted values, and unmanaged emotions took her life. She spent her entire life running from—even hiding from—fear, anxiety, and a lack of self-esteem. She never really "loved" herself. She looked for love and happiness from others. That lack of self-love caused pain. I concluded that to numb her pain, my mom turned to alcohol.

Throughout her life, my mother never felt "enough." She never *had* enough, and she never *was* enough. Growing up, my sister and I always heard this message and even internalized it ourselves to some degree. After her death, I found myself examining my own life, beliefs, values—and my self-worth.

On the outside, I looked like a success. As a teenager, I got a lot of attention in sports, show choir, marching band, and academics (when I tried hard enough). While I found temporary worthiness through the approval of others, I lacked self-confidence. I didn't like myself unless others liked me. Even though I got "attention" from everyone else, I still craved self-love, which no outsider—including my mom—could give me. Of course, at the time, I didn't understand what was really going on with me. I just knew I continually felt fearful and anxious and like I was playing the role of someone else.

I believe that my mother loved me as much as she was capable of loving me. I certainly felt loved by her. I did observe, however, that my mom's favorite activity with me and my sister was to go shopping. She bought us a lot of stuff, even though she would first tell us, "We don't have money for that." After the purchase, she would then say, "Don't tell your dad." Buying things for us made her happy, even though later she would stress about money. I think she bought stuff for us because she was filling a need from her past, a feeling that there was never enough, including the reality that her parents seldom could afford to take her shopping or buy her things. She wanted to please us and wanted us to like her, so she spent money she didn't have. Thinking about that now makes me feel sad.

I still carry memories of feeling financially insecure, of thinking my family could run out of money. I remember wanting to eat at restaurants with my mom but being told, "We can't afford that." I drove the worst car at my high school and was even voted "worst car" in our yearbook. People would laugh at me driving that car. It was embarrassing as hell. My dad told me I was lucky to even have a car. Dad talked about the importance of saving money. I took that to mean he just wanted to save it and not spend it; Mom spent it when she didn't have it to spend. This focus on money drove me crazy.

I decided I needed to make a lot of money, as clearly that would solve every problem. I focused on building financial wealth, which I was sure would then buy me self-worth, and peace. As a fear-driven young female, I did everything I could to build lots of money. How do you build money? You learn about money. You learn which jobs make a lot of money.

I had a friend who was a financial advisor. He was making over $100,000 a year working three days a week. I didn't need to hear much more. I just thought, "Sign me up." That is how I found my career as a financial advisor.

So . . . for twenty years I have built wealth for myself and others. I've worked hard, and each year I've increased my income and had plenty of money to support my life, my needs, and lots of wants for me and my family. And yet, I still felt it wasn't enough.

Unfortunately, it took me years—and my mother's death—to realize money alone doesn't build worth, nor could money bolster the self-worth that I was still lacking. And so began my personal development search—which continues to this day.

I believe that when we live the best version of ourselves, we then give our best to others. We have become enlightened to our purpose in living and giving. That is what I call abundance. Fully living. Fully giving. I have the word "abundance" tattooed on my wrist as a daily reminder to set these expectations for myself so I can, in turn, offer my best self to others. I believe we have been placed on earth to live out our unique purpose and to serve others in our family and in our world. Growing and giving involves taking real action with our time, talents, and resources, including finances.

While I'm still on a journey to better myself, I have arrived at one crucial decision: that I am enough, and I do have enough.

# Introduction

I believe our world is in desperate need of change. So many of us are living in what I call a "wealth crisis," which I believe stems from a *worth crisis*. We don't give ourselves enough love, acceptance, and power to grow into our true best selves. Instead, we trap ourselves in fear, anxiety, and doubt. When we don't live in alignment as a whole person, we don't have the energy or positive mindset to earn the money we deserve. We hold ourselves back from creating the life we truly desire.

Since you're holding my book in your hands right now, you may be searching for something. Your life is not what you want it to be. You want to make a change. You want to improve your circumstances, elevate your lifestyle, make more money, or get more from the money you have. You may be experiencing fear and anxiety. Right? The problem is you just don't know where to start.

I know that feeling. Been there, multiple times. Most people have. Coming to a crossroads or hitting a brick wall can happen at any age or even several times in one person's lifetime. I'm here to assure you that you do have the capacity to make your life better. It will take some work, but I'm here to help you.

You might be wondering, "What makes Dawn Dahlby qualified to help me with my finances?" You are smart to question anyone who gives you advice about your money. I am a CERTIFIED FINANCIAL PLANNER™ (CFP®) and a Behavioral Financial Advisor (BFA™), a rare dual certification in the field of finance. Let me explain why this matters.

I began working with clients more than twenty years ago. In the beginning, I used the techniques that were taught to me in my CERTIFIED FINANCIAL PLANNER™ courses, which focused on the technical details of clients' comprehensive financial plans. I would present detailed recommendations for their investment portfolios, which I believed would grow their money. Time after time, as I ran through the details of these investments, I would see their eyes glaze over. They couldn't look more uninterested. Yet, these were the very same people who had told me that they were concerned about their money and their financial futures. In fact, many of my clients expressed serious fears that they would run out of money in their lifetimes. I was seeing a disconnect; I wanted to know why.

My gut told me that instead of presenting the spreadsheet and investment plan analysis, I should be helping them explore their relationship with money, their fears surrounding it, and their behaviors regarding spending and saving. I realized that something in the way I interacted with clients needed to change. I needed to learn more about each client as a whole person before I started delving into their finances.

My mother named me Dawn for a reason, I think, because it was as if a bright light shone on the necessity of a new direction for me. Even with uncertainty, I still somehow found the courage to break free from my training and tackle something new by approaching my job from a new angle. I felt a fresh excitement about my work even though I had no idea at the time of all the learning I had ahead of me, both personally and professionally.

I began to spend more time in conversation with each client, listening deeply to his/her anxieties and concerns about money and what he/she really wanted to do with it. Each person thought about money differently: one wanted to be able to travel, another to leave something behind for his children, another just to feel secure that it would be there for her if needed. How could I help them achieve these goals? I concluded that I needed a process to follow with all clients that would begin by having them clarify their beliefs, values, and goals—for themselves and for me.

I realized that in order to best serve the whole-life needs of my clients, I needed to take my financial practice in a new, uncharted direction. This direction must combine the aspirations, behaviors, and emotions of my clients with the technical aspects of building their wealth. Again, I wanted to create a unique process that would meet clients where they were at the start of our relationship and from there help them meet the goals they hadn't even set yet. I investigated and discovered resources that educated me in this new direction. I became the first advisor in the country to earn the Behavioral Financial Advisor certificate.

I learned that money and emotions are not a good combination. When we are highly emotionally charged, it is not a good time to make any financial decisions. For example, you have a bad day at work, you feel defeated, and you decide to stop at the mall to decompress. Instead of buying just that latte, you decide you *deserve* a pair of shoes that are double the price you would normally pay. You justify your purchase as dealing with the difficulties at work, and you charge those shoes on your credit card!

The end of the month comes, and you can't pay the full credit card balance. The next few months pass and with some extra, unexpected expenses charged, you still can't pay off your card. Before you know it, many months turn into years of credit card debt, and you have now paid three times the price of those shoes that you don't even like anymore.

I also decided that I wanted the designation of "fiduciary" added to my identity as a financial advisor. Don't feel badly if you don't know what the heck a fiduciary is. Many people don't. However, anyone who works with a financial advisor should know whether he or she is working with a fiduciary. Why? Here's the deal. I am like a doctor who takes the Hippocratic Oath to do no harm. Legally, as a fiduciary, I must give each client the "best advice" for his/her financial situation. I am obligated to look for the best-quality, lowest-cost investment(s). Clients can trust that I am making the best investment choices for their portfolios, not for my financial benefit. Every decision I make on their behalf, every strategy I choose for them, must benefit them, not just earn me a bigger paycheck. I believe I earn my clients' trust by telling and showing them that my compensation is linked only to their financial growth. I only gain when they do.

Once I attained these further certificates, I felt equipped and empowered to change the content and style of my client meetings. As a result, these meetings improved significantly. Rather than the previous approach where I presented the alpha, beta, and standard deviations of clients' investment portfolios, I focused instead on their financial concerns and what kept them awake at night. I centered discussions with my clients around the psychology of their values, beliefs, and emotions involving not only their finances but their lifestyles in general. I began to focus on their individual needs—their priorities, their habits of spending and saving, their financial goals for their future—as central to any financial plan we created together. My process was evolving.

After sitting in thousands of client meetings and each time presenting a client's individual financial analysis, I realized that most clients in some way actually feared money. They feared not having enough money for today and for tomorrow. Almost none of them were able to achieve both freedom and security, which I believe are the two most important aspects of living a wealthy life—that is, having "spending freedom" today as well as financial security for tomorrow.

Many clients had healthy incomes, which provided them spending freedom—they didn't have to worry about the cost of everyday purchases. Still, they lacked security because they didn't have financial plans that would show them the results of their spending decisions and how they impacted their long-term financial goals. Or, they had financial security, meaning they put more value on saving for their future at the "expense" of not spending today. They feared running out of money in the future.

In nearly all cases, a client's relationship with money was based on fear—fear of overspending or oversaving. I wanted desperately to help clients banish their fears and allow them to experience both spending freedom and financial security.

I also discovered that for most of us, our "money" beliefs begin with our parents' thoughts and behaviors conveyed through both nonverbal and verbal communications. Many of my clients' parents had lived through significant adversity and had faced devastating scarcity. As a result, these clients were continuing practices they had either been taught or observed, such as washing out plastic sandwich bags, saving Christmas bows, and attempting to repair anything and everything in need of fixing.

These people, like their parents, had zero tolerance for waste—of food or of possessions. They lived their lives with this "scarcity" mindset. These conscientious people had spent their entire working lives saving money as though the depression was either continuing or was looming. They entered retirement living their same limiting habits, not allowing themselves the joy and satisfaction of spending their hard-earned money.

Through our interactions, I was also able to weave in and to share my evolving philosophy that living a life of worth and wealth is not just about becoming rich in dollars and cents to spend and save. Living a life of worth and wealth is about creating balance in our unique lives—balance between earning and spending, saving and giving, working and playing. It is about achieving personal and financial security. I believe when we live with both internal security (confidence in our own capabilities) and external security (what you value that money can buy), living for today and planning for tomorrow, we will have found happiness—true worth and true wealth.

This behavioral approach improves an individual's emotional competency and decision-making behavior in many aspects of life. It also results in the creation and management of more realistic and effective financial plans for individual clients because each client's needs and circumstances are unique.

## REAL-LIFE CLIENT EXAMPLES

The following are some short scenarios based on clients who have come to me for advice. Can you identify with any of them?

### Always Broke

Maria and Sam came to me with this question: "Why do we always feel broke? We have decent incomes, but we can't seem to find money to save." After much analysis of this couple's income, expenditures, and savings, along with their values and priorities of spending, we found that Maria and Sam were not using their income in a beneficial way. They had overspent on their new house; they had a mortgage payment that was too high a percentage of their budget. They had two kids in multiple activities that were costing them a significant amount of money each month, yet they considered this expense a priority. They were leading busy lives with minimal down time, so they spent a lot of money dining out. They also both drove expensive cars.

## Wants More

Kari was upset about her current income as a schoolteacher. She believed she was making a third less than all her friends, while putting in a third more time. Kari was exhausted but saw no way out. She loved her work but wanted a lifestyle that gave her more time and money—to spend and to save.

## Disappointed in Investments

Michael and Marcie came to me while in their thirties. They each had incomes that allowed them a lifestyle they really enjoyed. They wanted me to know that they add to their investments once a year, relying on their advisor to select those investments. However, they questioned why they were not seeing more growth in their investments.

## How I Helped These Clients

I could write hundreds more scenarios like these. The point is that you are not alone. Here's how I helped these clients.

After "Always Broke" Maria and Sam reset their priorities, they reiterated their support for their children's activities, but they agreed they could trade in both cars without feeling a big pinch. The Audi was replaced by a Mazda and the Lincoln was traded for an older version of the model that still had an extended warranty. They also agreed to reduce the number of meals out each month. They realized even more savings when they refinanced their home. These cost-reduction measures saved the couple $600 per month. After ten years, they not only had more usable income each month, but they turned their savings into over $100,000 in investments!

After analyzing "Wants More" Kari's core values, strengths, and purpose, she and I determined that she did need more income to support her life's desires. We looked at what she loved to do in her current job. She then looked for a career that would use her skills and passions. She landed a new career in corporate sales training where she could lead and teach— and that doubled the income she had been earning. Over the years, she still missed working with the younger generation, so she decided to host four complimentary workshops that she called "Learning Life Skills" every year for the teen children of the parents she was training.

I reviewed Michael and Marcie's current portfolio of "Disappointed in Investments." I discovered that their investments were performing like they should. In fact, they were slightly outperforming the benchmarks. Through conversations with these clients, I was able to point out that their investment behavior was sporadic. They would dump a sum of money into random investments during bonus time. However, they weren't saving enough to meet their long-term financial vision because they believed they could only afford to save when their yearly bonuses were paid out, rather than putting aside money each month throughout the year.

After assisting them with analyzing their spending and their investment portfolio, together we came up with a plan where they could afford to save a specific amount on a regular basis in the wisest investment for them. They were nervous about this plan at first, but after they had implemented it for several months, they realized they didn't even miss that amount of their monthly income. They also told me the most important part of this plan was knowing I was there as a partner to hold them accountable to their goals. When life threw them expensive curveballs, they called me. With non-emotional decision-making regarding their expenses, we reworked their spending plan to solve their short-term money issues while still holding tight to their long-term investment plan.

These are just a few of the hundreds of success stories of clients I've helped over the years. I will share many more throughout this book. I'm confident that by leading you through a sequential process, I will help you to achieve the change you need. If you feel the urgent need to pursue a specific subject, check out my chapter titles and feel free to turn to one of them immediately. However, I urge all my clients to trust the progressive process that I share here, which has brought wealth to me and also to my clients. Now, YOU are my client via the pages of this book. Let me guide you step by step along this proven path.

## EVERYTHING BEGINS WITH YOUR MINDSET

I love to feel happy. I love to be around happy, positive people. I love to make other people happy. I want to help you be a happy, healthy, wealthy person. Honestly, for that to happen, first you must understand and believe that you have unlimited power and potential. You can be, have, and do most anything you desire if you master your thinking by challenging your beliefs, manage your emotions through self-awareness, and act while aligning all aspects of your life.

You are the author writing your own story. Your story unfolds based on the thoughts and actions of your past and present. Your next chapter begins right now. Congratulations on taking this brave step.

Dealing with money does matter to your life, your well-being, and your ability to be happy. It starts not with your annual income or the amount of money presently in your bank accounts, it begins with your mindset. I like that word, but I use it carefully. Let me explain. According to Dictionary.com, "mindset" is "a fixed attitude, disposition, or mood." That word "fixed" is extremely important. If you are fixed, set, or stuck in an unhealthy, unproductive way of thinking and behaving, that's not helpful to you. If, however, you are "set" on beliefs, attitudes, and behaviors that are leading you to a happier, more fulfilled, self-confident, and constructive lifestyle, that's positive for you. I plan to help you analyze your unique mindset so you can check its efficacy in your life.

# KEY TERMS BEFORE WE START

Over the years, I have come to have a great respect for the meaning of words. Even more importantly, I strongly believe that in any conversation of significance, it is vital for the participants to agree on the meanings of the words they are using. Agreement on meaning brings clarity and understanding to the dialogue—though not necessarily agreement on the topic. This is where the conciliatory "agree to disagree" resolution might result.

Therefore, since you will be "writing" your own future and I want to assist you in that endeavor, it is essential that we agree on the meaning of key terms I will be using throughout this book. It is fairly common practice throughout our lives to consult a dictionary for the commonly held meanings of words. We've been doing this since childhood. Many of us learned early on that words not only can have various meanings, but often society has put various "spins" on those meanings.

I hope the following definitions and explanations will seem perceptive, pertinent, and practical. Perhaps you will even experience some "Aha" moments as you consider them.

## Defining Wealth

The Dictionary.com definition of "wealth" that I like is "an abundance or profusion of anything; plentiful amount." So, wealth encompasses more than money. Gaining wealth involves continuing personal and professional growth, deepening relationships, and creating a more meaningful, full life—"meaningful" and "full" as each person defines it, as you define it. In my opinion, wealth in the fullest sense of the word is the definition of happiness.

## Defining Worth

Again, I turn to Dictionary.com and two of the definitions that have influenced my philosophy. Worth is "excellence of character or quality as commanding esteem," and "usefulness or importance, as to the world, to a person, or for a purpose." My interpretation of those meanings is that "worth" indicates an individual has earned high self-esteem and a sense of internal personal security, and, in that earning process, has been a benefit to self and others.

## Determining Beliefs and Values

Do you know how powerful your beliefs, your convictions are? How about your values, or what is most important to you?

These beliefs and values determine your attitudes and behaviors, or at least they should. They affect how satisfied you are with yourself and your life. So, what are the beliefs you have acquired, the values you have chosen for your life in general and regarding your money specifically?

I believe that if any person is living with his or her true beliefs and values in alignment with his or her attitudes and behaviors, that individual is living a life of worth and wealth, and yes, happiness. Contrarily, a person who is not living a life in which beliefs, values, attitudes, behaviors, and goals are all in sync is confused, unsettled, unfulfilled, and insecure. This person is surely searching, perhaps even longing.

I can personally attest to interacting with such unhappy people, seeing firsthand the adage that "money can't buy happiness." If the person's values and behaviors aren't compatible, no amount of money will bring the individual inner peace, pride, contentment, self-confidence, or happiness. And, such people usually aren't easy to work or live with because they aren't reliable, genuine, or secure.

Money cannot buy worth. As for myself, I may still be a work in progress, but I know I strive to be a person of worth and wealth, a woman who walks her talk.

## WHERE IS THE STARTING POINT?

The quick answer is **you**! You are the starting point of this worth and wealth process.

When you elected to buy this book, I suspect that your interest might simply have been to learn how to have more money. This could include desiring information about a comprehensive financial plan, understanding good and bad debt management, or learning how to invest or how to minimize taxes. I promise, I'll get to all those topics. First, however, I want to emphasize that growing total worth is about aligning all that is you. It's about living life and creating a relationship with money according to what matters most: your core values, your belief systems, and your personal and professional purpose.

I believe you and I want to design our lives to reach the ultimate goal of total wealth and worth in every sense of the meaning of these rich words. What that looks like is unique to each individual, but we can all use a similar process for getting there.

What makes you unique? It's the sum of your values, beliefs, strengths, weaknesses, goals, purpose, personality, and experiences. And, the way you live your life—your decisions and actions—reflects all of those. When all these facets work together in harmony, your life is good. You have worth and wealth. You have freedom and security.

What you will not have is emotional pain. You will no longer experience guilt when spending your money differently than someone else. You will stop comparing your "lack of money" to someone else's "so much money." You will no longer fear the arrival of your credit card statement. There will be no dread of your emotions sabotaging your financial decisions. There will be no anxiety as you assess your savings in terms of future security. That anxiety can really take a toll on a person's body. I believe strongly that physical pain can result from emotional pain. Dealing with the latter may very well also ease the former.

## HOW THIS BOOK IS ORGANIZED

Part One of this book is going to take you through the vital steps of analyzing yourself and determining, at this moment in your life, your beliefs, values, and goals. Yup, this will take some time and effort. You may need to do some real soul-searching to answer this question: Is the way I am currently living my personal and work life reflecting what I have determined are my values, beliefs, and goals? Tough question, huh? Don't be surprised or discouraged if you don't find alignment. I didn't when I started in this business, and many of my clients didn't either. But I found that I could learn. I could change, and so can you.

Money is a tool for building your life, a tool to be used efficiently and effectively to construct the life you want, the kind of wealth you want. To properly live in your "true wealth," including financial, you need a plan with consistency and discipline, yet one that allows the fluidity necessary to address inevitable changes in your life. Though I do so with a chuckle, I agree with Warren Buffett, who once said, "An idiot with a plan can beat a genius without a plan."[1]

Yes, you need a plan! You need a process. Building wealth happens through your consistent positive actions which compound. Building worth happens through your handling of life's challenges in a way that produces positive change and growth.

---

1   This quote has been attributed to Warren Buffett. "'An Idiot with a Plan' – Warren Buffett [720×642]," QuoteThee, accessed December 24, 2018, https://www.quotethee.com/an-idiot-with-a-plan -warren-buffett-720x642/.

# BUILD WEALTH AND WORTH TOGETHER

When you gain wisdom and expertise through growing worth and wealth, you become the best version of yourself; you make the best decisions with your money and other resources. It is by working on your worth through personal development and learning the most important keys to building wealth that you gain the wisdom to live in complete alignment, through thoughts and actions. You then spread that wisdom to others through your joy of living. You become an example of how a life plan works. One by one our world starts to change. This is true abundance . . . living and giving. Seeking alignment requires making choices first, then taking action.

This "taking action" part can be very challenging, especially when you are lacking direction, energy, motivation, and goals. It's not easy to think and act differently, to get out of your comfort zone. Even if you are UNcomfortable in your "comfort zone," at least you're familiar with the feeling. I get it! Our brains are wired to resist change, so it can cause us distress to think and do things in a new way. Gaining knowledge, practicing skills, supporting each other, and *then* achieving success is when change becomes more desirable, and easier.

I want you to feel empowered to take charge, to take action, and to recreate your life. "I am convinced that life is 10 percent what happens to me and 90 percent how I react to it."[2] I believe this to be 100 percent true.

**Real wealth and worth are built from the inside out.**

---

2  Charles R. Swindoll, "Charles R. Swindoll Quotes > ," Goodreads, accessed July 2022, https://www.goodreads.com/author/quotes/5139.Charles_R_Swindoll.

## IT'S YOUR TURN

Okay, I can hear you thinking, maybe even saying out loud, "Hey, Dawn, more money would do a lot to help me."

Most people feel that way. However, recent research polling people with all different wealth levels, from those in poverty all the way up to billionaires, asked them this question: "How much is enough money?" No matter what financial demographic people were in, they all wanted "a little bit more." Even the billionaires!!![3] So, what does this tell us?

More money doesn't truly fill all the gaps within ourselves. Maybe people looking for "a little bit more money" are really searching for something else, something more—a feeling of more worth. It is my belief that people who feel more self-worth definitely have more wealth! I'm talking of wealth in the broadest sense—of a rich and fulfilling life—not limited to financial wealth. I'm talking about becoming WELLthy.

Do you really *need* more money, or do you just *want* more money? It's certainly acceptable to want more money left for recreation or saving after you've taken care of your needs. You just need to be aware of the choices you will have to make. I hope you will always keep your core values in mind when making those choices.

Think about what you need more money for. You may want to look for ways within your current day-to-day living in which you could make wiser choices with the money you earn. Then again, is it really more money you desire—or more satisfaction? Perhaps you are looking for more freedom in your lifestyle. Maybe you have concluded that your pursuit of money through your present job is giving you little free time to enjoy other things. It may seem that your current job controls you rather than you controlling its part in your life.

---

3    "Just a Little Bit More," *Starwinar* (blog), accessed July 2022,
     https://starwinar.wordpress.com/daily-short-story/just-a-little-bit-%20more/.

Are you ready to face these issues? I'd love to delve into them with you. Are you ready to start the process, your journey toward increased worth and wealth? If so, I'm with you.

## LET'S TAKE A WALK

Let's start with what I call "my walk down memory lane." Take some time to think about your past or even write out your story. Why? This exercise will help you understand what you were taught to believe about success, happiness, wealth, money, achievement, and self-esteem. There is so much value in writing down your past script.

You will likely begin to see patterns of behavior. Here are some questions to consider:

- Are you a risk-taker, or are you ultra-conservative with money?

- Are you led by your wants?

- Do you buy things before you have the money and then wishfully hope the money will follow?

- Do you define "wealth" only as having money?

As you take your memory walk, you may realize you are a planner or that you are living your life by default—believing that what happens, happens. Ponder mistakes that could have been avoided if you had taken more time to think actions through versus making emotional decisions. When I went through this process, I learned so much about myself. Many of my past decisions were driven by negative emotions, which took me down a path driven by fear.

Whether you have fully or partially reviewed your past, do you feel ready to start your journey toward increased worth and wealth? Don't worry if this seems like an overwhelming task; I'm here to help, just as I have helped many other people embark on this journey.

I want nothing more than for you to go on this life-transforming journey so you can witness the ripple effect in your life and the lives of others. You must start right where you are now—at this moment in your life. It can be a new beginning.

Come with me to *Part One—Own It!*

# Own Your Worth

## CHAPTER 1

# Starting with the Basics

We begin at the beginning. When you want to master anything new, from cooking to decorating to managing finances, you must start with the basics. You must start where you are currently, with what you already know and can do, and then build from there. In part one, *Own Your Worth*, I believe the basics involve figuring out what you value and believe. The basics require identifying your strengths and understanding which emotions and passions drive you. Last, but certainly not least, is determining what you believe is your life's purpose—the reason you are here now, and what you want to do with your time on this planet.

I will walk you through each of these basics in a general way and then lead you through exercises that will help you personalize them to your own needs. Always, the starting point is YOU.

## VALUES

A value is something extremely *valuable* to you, so important to you that you can't imagine living your life without it. It also means that people who know you well can identify your values from observing your behavior. You live what you value!

Over the years, I have come across many lists of values and exercises to help an individual identify those most important to him or her. To assist you, I have chosen to modify an exercise called "Think2Perform Values Exercise," by Doug Lennick.[4] Using the program's six-step process, you will determine your core values and define them in a way that is most "real" for you.

WARNING!

This is a challenging exercise. It will require time and focus. Grab your favorite beverage, search out a private, comfortable location, leave your cell phone behind, and let your loved ones know that you'd appreciate some "me" time.

Here is a list of twenty-five values with descriptors. Just slowly read through them before beginning your first step.

___Authenticity: honesty, sincerity, ethics

___Empathy: compassion, affinity, warmth

___Spirituality: faith, religion, devotion

___Gratitude: thankfulness, recognition, appreciation

___Health: fitness, well-being, beauty

___Contentment: tranquility, peace, calm

___Wisdom: knowledge, intelligence, understanding

___Loyalty: fidelity, allegiance, trust

___Relationships: friendship, association, network

___Generosity: service, altruism, charity

---

4   Think2Perform is a consulting firm offering "professional coaching, leadership consulting, and business development services." If you would like to do the original t2p Values Exercise, you can do so online for free at www.think2perform.com. "What Do You Value? Find out," Think2Perform, accessed July 2022, https://www.think2perform.com/our-approach/values.

___Ambition: attainment, achievement, distinction

___Leadership: guidance, direction, inspiration

___Reputation: fame, recognition, status

___Growth: improvement, progress, goal-oriented

___Competence: skill, knowledge, mastery

___Performance: achievement, success, hard work

___Dependability: accountability, trustworthiness,
reliability

___Organization: structure, order, function

___Security: protection, risk-aversion, reliability

___Balance: harmony, calmness, steadiness

___Adventure: exploration, spontaneity, action

___Enthusiasm: energy, eagerness, optimism

___Passion: intensity, emotional, devotion

___Individuality: independence, autonomy, uniqueness

___Imagination: creativity, originality, curiosity

(You may have noticed that "happiness" and "money" are not included in the above list. I believe that "happiness" is the result of living according to one's values. "Money" is a means to the end of living out one's values. More about this later.)

## Action Steps

Now that you've read through the list of values, I'm going to lead you step by step toward a list of your clear, specific, and very personal core values.

1. Check the fifteen values from the above list that must be included in your life for you to be happy and fulfilled. Take plenty of time with this. These may or may not be values instilled in you as a child. They

must be your adult values: values you choose to live by, descriptors of what is most important to you. There is no such thing as a right or wrong value. There are only the right values for you.

2. As if that wasn't a difficult enough task, of those fifteen, choose your most important ten. I'm not trying to have you drop the other values in your life, but I am "forcing" you to really analyze and prioritize. Ask yourself, "Which ten values must I have in my life to be who I want to be?"

3. Ready for the maximum challenge in this exercise? Of those ten, which five are your personal core values? In other words, choose the five values you wouldn't want to do life without. These are vital for you to identify because the vast majority of your future decisions and choices will be based on these five values.

List your top five values here:

_____

_____

_____

_____

_____

4. Now let's personalize your values a bit further. You need to add clarity and personal meaning to each of your five core values. Add your own descriptors, in words, phrases, or sentences. Here's why: many of us may list the same or similar values, but our definition of a stated value may be significantly different from that held by others. Let me explain further.

5. You may list "health" as a core value. "Health" to one person may refer to maintaining one's physical health only, to stay free of illness,

to be religious about labs, exams, immunizations, medications. To another, health may refer to maintaining mental or emotional health through counseling and/or medications. Someone else may equate health with beauty and staying youthful, using products and procedures. Still others may consider exercise, healthy eating, massages, meditation, or communing with nature as essential components of their "health." Some would choose a combination of these.

6. For example, if "relationships" is one of your values, what is it about relationships that you find truly meaningful? Specify relationships you value the most. State "feeling close" to your spouse, children, grandchildren if your priority is spending time with them. List getting together regularly with friends to chat over coffee or a glass of wine if that is your value. Perhaps your more accurate desire is having deep intellectual conversations with others, having friends to travel with, or spending social time with colleagues outside of work.

7. Write down each value and the descriptors, the definition you would use for that value.

Value #1: _____

To me, this value means _____

Value #2: _____

To me, this value means _____

Value #3: _____

To me, this value means _____

Value #4: _____

To me, this value means _____

Value #5: _____

To me, this value means _____

8. Go deeper now and add in your "whats" and your "whys." It's fine if this exercise is messy. You may change your mind and choose different values or start with one definition or rationale and end up with something different later, such as an explanation that more accurately describes what is important to you. What matters is that you assign definitions to your values so that they are crystal clear in your mind. This will help you understand why each value is so important to you.

9. Take each of your five defined core values and explain why this value means so much to you, why it is essential to your happiness. I'll give you plenty of space for each of your five core values.

Core Value #1: _____

This value is essential to my happiness because _____

_____

_____

_____


Core Value #2: _____

This value is essential to my happiness because _____

_____

_____

_____


Core Value #3: _____

This value is essential to my happiness because _____

_____

_____

_____

_____

Core Value #4: _____

This value is essential to my happiness because _____

_____

_____

_____

_____


Core Value #5: _____

This value is essential to my happiness because _____

_____

_____

_____

_____


10. Lastly, decide if you are truly ready to own these values. If not, take some more time to identify and describe your core values and why living them is essential to your happiness. I promise, you'll soon understand why being clear about your values is so essential to achieving your wealth and worth. Remember, our values tend to dictate our choices and our behavior. They're such an integral part of our life that even our friends should be able to identify these values by the way we live our lives.

Congratulations on completing this exercise on values. Whether you have been aware of it or not, you can now see that your values enter every aspect of your life and that some are stronger than others. I believe you will find that being clear about what you value will make it easier to make decisions and to understand when you run into relationship and job-related conflicts.

Consider that when you disagree or have a conflict with a family member, friend, or colleague, it's usually because both of you have a different set of values and beliefs, at least on the topic at hand. Usually, those who understand and respect the importance of other people's values can agree to disagree and then move on in their relationship. On occasion, however, different values simply do not work well together, and therefore, neither does the relationship.

A client once told me that she had been married for fifteen years, but she and her husband continued to have ongoing marital problems. Reluctantly, her husband accompanied her to see a counselor, who took them through a core values exercise similar to the one you just completed. At the end of the activity, they both shared their top five values. Only one of their core values was the same. It became painfully clear why they were struggling: they didn't share the same values and therefore didn't have common goals or a joint vision for their future. To their credit they continued with further counseling, but within a year or so, they decided to amicably divorce.

I'm sure you can understand why I believe discussing core values is much better entered into in the early days of a potentially serious relationship—rather than after the wedding. Never make assumptions around a loved one's values. Communicate about them.

Decision-making becomes much easier the clearer your values are in your mind. Suppose you have determined that relationships, that is, spending quality time with your children, are most valuable to you. So, a friend calls with free tickets to a concert you've wanted to attend but thought was way too expensive. You have already told your child that you will be "front and center" at his sixth-grade band concert. For a few seconds you fight an internal battle, then thank your friend for thinking of you and smile as you imagine watching your son proudly play his tuba.

When faced with a decision of almost any magnitude, if we return to our core values, the choice we must make becomes apparent.

## DAWN'S STORY—MY FAITH

In the spirit of being transparent, I want to share my number-one value. I include this with total respect that you may not share this value with me. In this book, there will be no attempt on my part to try to make my values yours. However, in teaching you about values and their giant part in achieving your own worth and wealth, I maintain that values will direct your goal setting and decision-making. My values direct mine.

My number-one core value is spirituality, my faith. I believe in God, who created me, loves me, and wants me to be the best me I can be, which is exactly what I want.

If I were doing the previous exercises, I would say that for me, faith represents belief in God and looking to the Bible for wisdom. When it comes to making complex decisions, for example, rather than quickly formulating standardized client plans, I choose to take the time to analyze all options. I present them to clients for their input, and I revise plans until the clients and I have arrived at the most effective individualized plans. I rely on my faith to keep my focus on my clients' needs, not my own financial gain.

I think you would agree that life is full of uncertainty which, in turn, can cause us to live in fear. The fear of the unknown is scary. Doing the right thing can be difficult. However, what I have learned from studying my top core value of faith is that if I really want to create certainty and consistency in my life and have clear direction, I must trust in God for guidance in the use of my ability, knowledge, and skills. I commit to doing what is right for the clients I serve. In doing so I live in peace and abundance—as do my clients.

Again, this is my top value and what it means to me. You are not me. You are you. Any attempt on our part to compare ourselves to others or to lead a life that doesn't fit us will only lead to feelings of discontent and failure. I certainly can learn and grow with you, but I must create a life unique to me, and you one unique to you. So, look at your values once again. Be proud to own your values.

## BELIEFS

The values people hold are often intertwined with their beliefs as well as with their convictions, ideas, and ideals. For example, if I say competence is very important to me, then I probably believe it is important for me to spend a significant amount of time perfecting my skills, attending classes and seminars in my profession, or maybe even earning certifications or a specific degree. Additionally, I may believe that my success in attaining competence is measured in money earned, while another person may believe that his or her success should be measured by the recognition received or by the free time gained.

**Your beliefs guide your growth.**
**Update them so you don't limit your potential.**

Your beliefs about yourself should give you the confidence to set new or higher goals for yourself, not keep you as a victim of life's circumstances. You may want to analyze the beliefs you grew up with. You'll probably find some you choose to hang on to, while you let go of others.

In *The Biology of Belief,* Dr. Bruce Lipton claims that "stunning new scientific discoveries about the biochemical effects of the brain's functioning show that all the cells of your body are affected by your thoughts."[5] He also believes that we develop our beliefs about life, including money, very early in life, during our formative years.

---

5    Bruce H. Lipton, *The Biology of Belief.* (London: Hay House), 2005.

There is evidence that we form most of our subconscious beliefs between conception and age six. Pretty early in a person's life, for sure! Assuming this is true, then surely your beliefs about how life and money work were formed from your parents' beliefs and how they put those beliefs into action in your family of origin. If, like me, you lived in a blended family, you were exposed to even more varied beliefs.

## Action Steps—Connecting Values and Beliefs

I have developed a simple method for discovering the beliefs that underpin and support our five core values. Use the lines below to further explore each of your values, the beliefs that emerge from each, and how a specific value and belief will be exhibited in your life. I will share a couple of my core values as a sample for you to follow.

> I, Dawn, value <u>FAITH</u>, so, concerning this value, I believe I have a God who loves me, who wants the best for me, and who will guide me through life.
>
> I am living this value by setting aside time to communicate with Him through prayer and meditation.
>
> I, Dawn, value <u>HEALTH</u>, so, concerning this value, I believe there is a strong connection between the food I eat, the exercise I get, a positive attitude, and my overall health and energy levels.
>
> I am living this value by eating healthy foods most of the time, exercising multiple times a week, and making time for meditation to focus my sometimes overactive, scattered mind so I can stay energized and positive.

Your turn . . .

I value _____

So, concerning this value, I believe _____

_____

_____

And I am/will be living this value by _____

_____

_____


I value _____ ,

So, concerning this value, I believe _____

_____

_____

And I am/will be living this value by_____

_____

_____


I value _____ ,

So, concerning this value, I believe _____

_____

_____

And I am/will be living this value by _____

_____

_____


I value _____ ,

So, concerning this value, I believe _____

_____

_____

And I am/will be living this value by _____

_____

_____

_____


I value _____ ,

So, concerning this value, I believe _____

_____

_____

And I am/will be living this value by _____

_____

_____

_____


While this is a challenging exercise, I guarantee that all these exercises to establish your values and beliefs are worth your time. One's self-esteem emerges from one's beliefs about self. What do you believe about yourself? As you deal with your finances, your beliefs about money reveal themselves. What do you believe about money? In order not to limit your potential, your wealth and worth, it is important to bring your beliefs into focus and be ready to change or revise them as you gain new insights into what you truly value.

In my own life, as I came to terms with my mother's death, I learned firsthand how our "inherited" and "hidden" beliefs can permeate our daily behaviors and prevent us from developing our full personal and professional potential. These beliefs seem to grow like weeds in a garden; even though you keep pulling them out, they continue to pop up over time. Recognize when you see a "weed" growing in your thinking and pull it out. It's only through awareness that we are able to change, grow, recreate, and redirect our values and beliefs.

Through awareness, limiting beliefs can completely lose their power.

## DAWN'S STORY—RELATIONSHIPS. WOE OR WOW?

One of my top five core values, which is a common one, is relationships. To me, a "relationship" involves having a deep connection with another person, whether a family member or a friend. To me, such a connection involves five components:

1. Similar thinking on a myriad of subjects
2. Sharing experiences and activities we find mutually enjoyable
3. Having deep, meaningful discussions on topics we deem important to us while trusting in confidentiality and respect
4. Feeling no sense of competition with this person
5. Looking for the humor in daily life

As a young adult, I believed I had a special relationship with my friend, Kendra. I believed she met all of my five requirements above. I loved to hang out with her. We could talk for hours about anything and everything. We went shopping, out for dinners, and laughed constantly when we were together. I considered her my BFF.

Over the next decade or so, time, distance, careers, spouses, and kids eventually invaded our relationship, and I saw our bond weakening. But honestly, it was more than that. It seemed that when we were together, fewer and fewer topics could be discussed comfortably. I realized that our values were no longer as closely aligned.

At times her judgments of my success gave off vibes of her insecurity or even jealousy. That hurt! Me picking up our dinner tab and giving her expensive gifts became expectations to her and obligations to me. We disagreed on how we spent and saved our money. One time she jumped all over me for buying an expensive name-brand purse. Foolishly, I took the bait and pointed out rather loudly that I owned one purse while she owned three or four. Why was I engaging in this frivolous debate? I had a right to spend my money the way I wanted, and she did also. Sadly, this relationship was deteriorating rapidly.

Time after time, I heard more and more negativity from her. My attempts at positivity were rejected. She was beginning to see herself as a victim; I saw her as unwilling to make changes. She tried, and often succeeded, to make me feel guilty for the income I earned and how I chose to spend my money. I had deeply loved this friend for so many years, but I began to regret how intimately I had shared with her. I no longer wished to continue this dysfunctional relationship. And, I felt guilty for feeling this way.

Yes, I shed tears over this loss for a time. I regretted some things I said to her out of great frustration. I felt guilty that in my professional success, I seemed to have failed a personal friendship. I prayed for insight and a solution. I tried expressing honest thoughts and emotions to Kendra, but I felt neither listened to nor understood. My attempts at resolution were dismissed or avoided. This drama continued for several years.

After long-overdue, honest self-evaluation, I concluded that I needed to move on. I felt sad about that, but I tried to banish the regret and guilt I felt. I had given that relationship my all. It was time to let go. And I did.

## STRENGTHS

We commonly assume that a strength is a positive quality of an individual, something a person is good at. Imagine my surprise when I turned to the dictionary for verification and found numerous definitions:[6]

- muscular power

- vigor

- mental power

---

6   "Strength," Dictionary.com, accessed July 2022, https://www.dictionary.com/browse/strength.

- moral power

- courage

- power by reason of influence, authority, resources, numbers

- effective force, potency, or cogency

- power of resisting force, strain, or wear

- something or someone that gives one strength or is a source of power or encouragement

I'm sure you were as struck with the repetition of the word "power" as I was. To me, this shows that a person's strength is a person's power. Your strengths are what empower you to make things happen for yourself and others. It's important to build on the personality traits, talents, abilities, skills you have already developed over the years. This is how you focus on your superpowers.

**Yes, you do have a superpower. Live yours fully.**

Yes, you do have a superpower—or several—and you need to live it fully. When you exercise your superpower, you build your worth. You feel comfortable being you. Instead of negatively comparing yourself to others, you celebrate one another's differences and strengths. Embracing and building upon your superpowers will allow you to make more money and become more of your unique self.

Take the time to write out all the strengths, the powers, you have. Be honest. What do you do really well? What skills and talents have you been complimented on over the years by teachers, bosses, family, and friends? This is not the time to be humble. Brag about yourself to yourself. If you need some validation, ask a few people closest to you for their perspectives.

You might start with the skills you bring to your work; you probably draw on your strengths every day.

Describe at least four of your superpowers.

1. _____

   _____

2. _____

   _____

3. _____

   _____

4. _____

   _____

This activity should be a confidence booster. You have identified four of your strengths and in doing so probably have thought of additional ones. That's good. Keep that going. So many of us tend to focus on our weaknesses—what we can't do.

Remember that you have developed these strengths with time and experience, with practice. That realization can motivate you to search for others of your qualities and skills that you would like to enhance. You can now see the possibilities for increasing the number of your superpowers, and with that, your self-esteem.

## WHAT I FOUND ABOUT MY OWN SUPERPOWERS

Learning about strengths in general and pinpointing my own in particular was a pivotal point in my personal and professional growth. I soon realized that identifying my strengths was one thing but living my professional life in alignment with those strengths would mean taking my career to a whole new level. I decided that playing to my strengths meant I should be utilizing them for at least 70 percent of my professional time. Likewise, I determined that I needed to spend 70 percent of my personal time living according to my core values.

Over the years, I've identified my strengths and incorporated them into my career. However, I believe I still haven't fully tapped into these gifts due to my own insecurities and fears, which I still battle at times. Yet the more I recognize and manage my fears, the more rewarding I find each day.

Here's how I set up my strengths/values alignment, which I keep on my desktop as a constant reminder of my superpowers and how I incorporate them into my lifestyle. It allows me to own my worth every day. By way of explanation, I have listed two of my values. Underneath these values are several descriptors to clarify what each value means to me. I listed my strength and several statements to further explain it. I added a conclusion to pull it all together.

| My Value | My Strength |
|---|---|
| Relationships | Winning over others |
| Making deep connections<br>Being with people<br>Seeking out similar mindsets | Building strong relationships<br>Influencing and inspiring<br>Networking |
| **Conclusion**: My strength is working with people and making strong connections with them to the point of influencing and inspiring them. This strength is very compatible with my value of forming relationships and seeking out people with whom I share interests and philosophy. Therefore, I need to focus my strengths on the clients I work with, my readers, and others open to my influence in order to help them all build worth and wealth. | |

| My Value | My Strength |
|---|---|
| Excitement | Positivity |
| Creating experiences<br>Having fun<br>Maintaining high energy | Focusing on the plus side of experiences<br>Enthusiasm<br>Exciting others |
| **Conclusion:** I am an enthusiastic, positive person who always seeks to have others join me in making lemonade when life gives us lemons. This positivity leads me to enthusiastically design educational and fun experiences for people in my personal and professional world. Therefore, I commit to energetically helping each person deal with his/her personal and financial challenges. | |

As you go through this exercise in the following charts, you will start to see themes and overlaps between your strengths and values. It will become clear how you should be spending your time and money. Fully utilizing your strengths on the job will help you grow your income faster and offer immeasurable work satisfaction. Spending time and money living out your values will help you become more fulfilled personally, will create an appropriate work/life balance, and will give you more zest for living.

## Action Steps—Aligning Values and Strengths

Now it's your turn to make your own values/strength chart as follows:

| My Value | My Strength |
|---|---|
|  |  |
|  |  |
| **Conclusion:** | |

*continued*

# Live WELLthy

| My Value | My Strength |
|----------|-------------|
|          |             |
|          |             |

**Conclusion:**

| My Value | My Strength |
|----------|-------------|
|          |             |
|          |             |

**Conclusion:**

| My Value | My Strength |
|----------|-------------|
|          |             |
|          |             |

**Conclusion:**

| My Value | My Strength |
|---|---|
|  |  |
|  |  |
| **Conclusion:** | |

# WEAKNESSES

In the spirit of keeping it real, I want to address weaknesses. Briefly. Go ahead and admit to a couple if you wish. (FYI: mine will be quite clear to you in the upcoming pages!)

Like it or not, we all know we have some weaknesses. For the most part, I see no point in focusing on those. Most of us are plenty hard on ourselves as it is. However, regarding weaknesses, here is my tip for you. If yours don't interfere with your values and beliefs, your family life, the requirements of your chosen work, no problem. Forget about them! However, if you think working on your weaknesses may improve your success in living your values and beliefs, personally and professionally, give some thought to how you might "fix" them.

## DAWN'S STORY—ADMITTING TO IMPATIENCE

I believe my biggest weakness is being impatient. I have an active mind, and throughout my entire life I have felt like everything in my daily routine was moving slower than my thoughts. It's super frustrating to live like this. I've always felt in a hurry to get somewhere.

*continued*

Relaxation to me equates to "sleeping." I've never allowed time for myself to relax during the day, but instead I take an extra hour at night, my "sleepy" time before actual sleep.

I've found that being impatient can be both beneficial and detrimental to growing a business, growing relationships, or aligning savings and spending. The beneficial part is that I want it now. I want success, money, a specific lifestyle, meaningful relationships. Impatience keeps me motivated to attain these.

The not-so-beneficial part is yes, you guessed it, I want it now! Yet a successful business, vibrant, trusting relationships, and wealth do not happen instantly.

Being impatient has served me well at times when a lot of tasks needed to be completed in a limited amount of time. At other times, however, my impatience has resulted in consequences I do not accept. My husband and two girls have become irritated with me numerous times when they approach me with a question or an issue, saying, "You never listen. You never have time."

I believe I have a legitimate objection to their use of the word "never"! However, I do realize I am very quick to brush them off if I am on a roll with an activity and/or if I instantly deem their "business" to be trivial. Ironically, my impatience often costs me more time than it saves, as I then have to deal with the anger, feelings of rejection, or rebellious behavior that have resulted. I should at least respectfully acknowledge their requests for my time. I either need to calmly explain why I cannot talk at the moment and add a sincere "Give me ten minutes and I'll sit down with you," or stop what I'm doing and listen right then.

True, my family needs to be sensitive to my agenda also. If I am in the middle of a phone call, or working on a video, then their need must be postponed and, to their credit, it usually is. I own that too often my impatience overrides my good intentions.

I want my family to know that I am approachable when they need me and that they are my number-one priority. To date, I have not fully managed my impatience. Remember, like the rest of the world, I'm still a work in progress!

The following are two other people's experiences dealing with their weaknesses.

## Kayli

Kayli has been recognized as a successful employee by her coworkers and supervisors. She recently earned a promotion to director. This new role will require her to hold meetings with employees, do some training, and conduct many personnel evaluations. She becomes anxious when put "in charge," a state clearly out of her comfort zone. Kayli could turn down the promotion, but she wants the increased pay and is extremely proud that her work ethic has been recognized.

When accepting the new position, she could ask her supervisor to help her improve her leadership and relationship skills through mentoring and modeling. Kayli could also take a course at a community college designed to help employees learn these skills. She could read books on this topic.

With some help, along with her already established skills, Kayli could go far in the company.

## Alec

Alec is very efficient and gets more work accomplished than most. But his strengths, if taken to the extreme, can actually become negatives. He was cautioned in an evaluation that occasionally in trying to work too quickly, he made costly mistakes or became impatient with his coworkers. Likewise, he was praised for his organizational skills but told that others on his sales team sometimes found him very controlling and felt like it was his way or the highway.

Alec had to make a choice. He could argue with his supervisor and ignore the input, or rethink and analyze his behaviors for future interactions. He could also talk with a trusted colleague and ask that individual to intervene with some silent cues when Alec wanders into sloppy, dictatorial, or controlling territory.

Alec definitely has desired competencies that he could turn into total positives. As soon as Alec gets past his defensiveness and focuses on the positive aspects of his evaluation, he can start making a concerted effort to behave differently in meetings. He could even set up regular "feedback" sessions with one of his teammates to check on his progress.

The experiences of Kayli, Alec, and me reveal not only weaknesses, but also the need to discuss concerns, issues, and fears with others. When considering your own weaknesses and how to get past them, reach out to people you trust for their perspectives and expertise. Bottling up emotions and thoughts can fill people with anxiety, and elevated emotions of fear, confusion, and regret can impact clear thinking.

Discuss your issues with others. You will learn, as I did, that your issues can turn into lessons. Use the personal and/or professional tribes you have in your life. You don't have to commit to following their advice, only to listening and considering their opinions and input. Please don't be embarrassed to share. In the end, you learn and often also teach others the value of consultation.

We all have weaknesses. Most people like and respect you more, not less, when you acknowledge your weaknesses and make efforts to correct them. Another benefit is that when you do that, you become more patient with and helpful to others struggling to be their best selves. Over the years, I have seen that individuals with high self-esteem welcome constructive criticism as well as accolades and turn both into growth and success. Don't let anything interfere with your superpowers.

**Acknowledging a weakness is a strength people respect.**

## EMOTIONS

There are those who believe that feelings like joy, sorrow, fear, hate, and love have no place in a discussion of the business of finances. Rather, rational cognitive skills are all that should be necessary in such matters.

Are you kidding me? You can't talk about being fully human without bringing in emotions. I'm sure you've heard all of these:

- "I love my job" (or "I hate my job").

- "I'm afraid I might lose my job."

- "I envy how much money my brother makes."

- "I feel such joy when I travel with my kids."

- "I hate spending every weekend doing yard work (or cleaning and laundry)."

Without revealing emotions, I don't think humans would be fully alive or fully living.

We are emotional creatures, like it or not. Think about it. Don't you agree that our first reaction to any situation is frequently an emotional one? We are wired that way. Emote, then think. Therefore, when it comes to emotions, the key is to identify and understand our emotions, learn how to express them appropriately, and then decide how to manage them. This sounds simple, but it's not. Most of us allow our emotions to control our behavior. Due to our emotional state, we often react without thinking. Can you relate?

Too many of us allow our emotions to manage us. That can get us into a lot of trouble. And worse, too frequently the emotion goes away much more quickly than the fallout from how we expressed it or a decision we made during that emotional state. Have you learned this from an experience of your own? I sure have.

## DAWN'S STORY—"MAN CAVE" DEBACLE

My husband and I had just moved into our "dream house" in Woodbury, Minnesota. My emotions of excitement and fear were flowing turbulently. All four of us were excited about our beautiful, brand-new living environment, but I was especially nervous about all the upcoming household expenses, including the new mortgage payment and property taxes.

I was so eager to move in, as I was absolutely obsessed with decorating, inside and out. My husband, on the other hand, was zeroing in on his "man cave," his very own movie theater. As an introvert, Gary treasures "Gary space," provided that space is filled with the newest technology designed to give the viewer the full home-theater experience.

After a few months of unpacking and living in the house, we started to find some time to make our new house a home. To me, making a house a home is about creating a warm, relaxing, but inspiring environment. One of my core values is excitement, which I translate to entertaining guests in our home. I love to create fun experiences with friends and family in well-designed environments. In contrast, one of my husband's core values is independence. To him this means finding peace and quiet, having "Gary time." Can you blame him? After all, he's living with three girls, two of whom are teenagers!

As the primary earner, I was very cognizant of our spending, of what we could and couldn't afford while making our house a home. One evening as I was hanging up some artwork, Gary stopped me and wanted to talk about getting a projector for his man cave. I hate to admit it, but my first words were, "How much does that cost?"

Gary knew exactly how much it would cost. However, knowing me, he decided to tell me an approximate range of what he "thought it would cost."

I replied, "Let's talk about it more and do some research to make sure we are getting the best deal." He took that as "Well, she didn't say 'no' so that must mean 'yes.'" Well, guess what? Within 48 hours or less, Gary came to me and told me that he had purchased the projector "because Best Buy was having a sale."

I literally freaked out at him, screaming at the top of my lungs, "We didn't discuss you buying the projector!"

He retorted, "But we did discuss it, and it was on sale."

All I could think was OMG! Now there would be this additional cost on top of everything else we *needed*! How were we going to afford all of this?

Of course, I had already mentally planned all the other expenses we had coming at us: the new blinds, new furniture, and of course, the mortgage payment. I was livid. I also thought, "Damn, I'm the one who makes all the money. I get to decide how we spend it." I did not speak to Gary for over a week.

Then, one night I was lying in bed with my computer, shopping for all the things we needed for our new place. I suddenly added up everything I wanted to buy and found that my "home decor" total was higher than the projector Gary had just purchased. None of the things that were in my virtual shopping cart were necessary or of immediate need.

This was when it hit me. Gary really didn't spend a lot of money on himself. He didn't shop for expensive shoes or purses; he didn't take expensive "guy" trips, and he certainly was always putting his family first. This man cave was important to him and if I didn't purchase what I wanted, it was 100 percent affordable for us. The projector he picked out was a very modestly priced one, a heck of a lot less expensive than all I had planned on purchasing.

When I was able to think rationally instead of emotionally about our different values and our different spending habits, I was able to see how I had overreacted with fear and selfishness. Especially selfish were my thoughts of who makes the money. I scolded myself, "We are a married couple, both contributing to the family. We make decisions together, not ones based on who makes the money."

Many of the upcoming expenses I had focused on were what I wanted. Yep, with my ears down and my tail between my legs, I went to tell Gary what I had just admitted to myself. We were then able to unemotionally discuss each of our contributions to this episode of faulty communication. And yes, I offered my apology for letting my emotions get the best of me.

*continued*

And we never, ever had any further communication issues. Yeah, right. Remember, I told you I'm a work in progress!

You shouldn't deny your emotions or your feelings, but you do need to learn to manage them. To do this, have a talk with yourself about what you're feeling and then beckon to your rational mind to choose how to react to that emotion. Take it from me, this takes lots and lots of practice (and sometimes counseling), but it is so worth the effort.

Acknowledged emotions followed by rational thoughts and sound choices of action make for constructive decision-making and fewer regrets. Managing one's emotions in a healthy way while making decisions is essential in all aspects of life, from communicating with a spouse to disciplining a child, from problem-solving with colleagues to creating a personal spending plan.

## Action Steps—Unpacking Emotions

Think about which emotions you most often express. Anger is probably high on that list as it's one of the quickest to jump to the forefront. Analyze your typical response when you feel angry, then determine if it is really anger you feel or if it is actually hurt, fear, or something else. Envy and jealousy can be stifling or result in us acting out in harmful, hurtful ways. However, such negative emotions can also push us into growth mode where we decide to react in more civil, mature, and beneficial ways. Acknowledging negative emotions and dealing with them can motivate us toward achievement. They can lead us to a positive outcome.

Many of us have trouble expressing love, gratitude, and joy. Take a moment to think about your emotional intelligence and your emotional competence as they apply to various day-to-day situations. Consider where you need the most work in becoming aware of your actual emotions and in managing them in a healthy manner. Answer the following questions as honestly and specifically as you can:

Am I aware of what I feel at any given moment?

_____

_____

Do I express my feelings in a healthy way? Why or why not?

_____

_____

Do I know the difference between healthy and unhealthy expressions of emotions?

_____

_____

Do I make decisions in my life from feelings or from rational thinking?

_____

_____

I realize these are some tough questions. I resisted answering them honestly myself for a long time, but I had to acknowledge that becoming a more mature and effective person meant changing the way I dealt with my own emotions. It required a shift in mindset and taking responsibility for the part I played in any given scenario.

For example, instead of saying, "My boss made me mad (so I talked behind her back all day)," choose a more productive approach by acknowledging, "I'm really angry with my boss right now. I don't have to deal with this today. Tomorrow I will schedule a meeting to talk with her and try to come to a better understanding." Be rational, not reactive.

**Managing your emotions gives you wisdom.**

# PASSIONS

My definition of passions is "emotions on steroids!" I maintain that my various passions contribute to my full, successful, happy life. Ask anyone close to me and they will tell you I have a passion for being center stage.

My dad tells the story that before I was even two years old, he caught me dancing on the tray of my highchair! I've loved to entertain ever since—as a front-row singer and dancer in high school show choir, the opening singing act at a resort out East, an entertainer on multiple cruise ships, a public speaker on personal finance, and the costumed host of many parties for family and friends.

Along with that, I have a passion for helping people, whether it's helping my daughters shop for clothes for a special dance, giving them advice on one of their dramas, taking a trip with a friend recovering from cancer, or creating a financial plan with an indebted couple.

I also love creating environments that meet other people's needs as well as my own. At my home I have created spaces for work and for play, for meditation and for conversation, for privacy and for partying, for indoor time and for outdoor time. I want people to be happy no matter the circumstances. That makes me happy. Currently, I feel I have incorporated aspects of all these passions as I author this book, create a website, serve as a guest speaker, and meet individually or in groups with clients. I'm busier than I've ever been, but because I am living my passions, I experience excitement, the joy of many cherished relationships, and the pride of achievement—three of my core values.

It's your turn.

Take that walk down memory lane once again. Think of the times when you felt fully alive. What was happening? You must have been doing something you love to do. As a child what were your first interests and passions? What did you want to be when you grew up? You may be satisfied that those early "dreams" are no longer relevant or desired, but don't be too quick with that decision. Such daydreams may deserve revisiting. The seeds of fulfillment in your adult life may have been sown from the traits acquired and joys experienced in your childhood and adolescence.

And now in your adult life, what makes you jump for joy? Or perhaps you aren't a "jump for joy" personality and think of "passions" a bit differently. What are you doing when you feel like "all's right in my world"? The passion of love can be expressed with hugs, kisses, and lovemaking, but also felt with a quieter intensity while watching your spouse playing "Old Maid" with your five-year-old, walking side by side through the park with a dear friend, or handing out bags of groceries to a homeless person at a food bank.

For an outgoing person like me, my passions aren't a secret to anyone who knows me, but others may feel equally passionate in a more subdued manner. Like with values, beliefs, and strengths that we live out in our unique way, what brings out the emotions, the passions in each of us, and how we display those are also unique to each of us. Let's see if I can help you become more aware of yours.

## Action Steps—Pinpoint Your Passions

I shared three of my passions with you and now encourage you to spend time reflecting on the following questions, which I hope will get you in touch with yours.

Write down the activities that you get excited about. What makes you super happy? How can others tell that you are experiencing this passion?

_____

_____

_____

_____

Describe the best times of your life. Imagine (on paper!) what it would take for you to experience such happiness in your present and future.

_____

_____

_____

If money didn't exist and you never had to work another day in your life, how would you spend your time?

_____

_____

_____

_____

_____

## PURPOSE

Now we get down to the final foundational basic. You've explored your values, beliefs, strengths, and passions. Now it is time to explore your purpose, which I believe incorporates all of these. Dictionary.com defines purpose as "the reason for which something exists." You and I exist for a reason—for a purpose. Purpose gives us direction.

You know, the word "unique" is used frequently by me and by others.

I am unique. You are unique. It is exciting to think about what this really means—there is absolutely no one on this planet exactly like me, nor exactly like you. No one in this world is going to "do life" exactly like me, nor exactly like you. During my time on earth, I will "be" and "do" in a way that impacts others, positively and/or negatively. I will exert my influence. This will happen regardless of whether my words and actions are unintentional or intentional.

I believe the same is true for you. Each of us makes an impact. Each of us influences. Things get interesting when individuals intentionally, purposefully impact and influence one another. How are you influencing others?

I do believe most people attempt to do work that is purposeful and that serves others, be that their families, friends, or the greater world. Believe me, this work is out there. Your work is out there. From personal experience, I maintain you won't find your purpose until you get right with yourself. You need to focus on building a life, not a living. When you build a life first, based on all that you are, the "living" or "money" will flow purposefully to you. If you don't live out your true calling, you will never be fulfilled.

**Focus on building a life, not just on making a living.**

As I have for previous topics, before I ask you to articulate your purpose, I will share mine. My purpose, and I suspect yours also, has changed over the years and continues to evolve to this day. As I admitted earlier, at the beginning of my career as a financial advisor, I certainly wanted to offer my clients the best advice and service I could with what I knew and believed at the time.

I also wanted to make money, lots of money. I wanted financial security for myself and my family. I wanted "stuff," too, as well as experiences and adventures with my husband, girls, and extended family and friends. At the time, I believed this was my purpose. I accomplished all of that. I enjoyed it all. I had fun. I worked super hard for my clients and with my colleagues to grow our business. We were successful, which was personally fulfilling and motivating. Still, I asked myself, motivating toward what end? Just so my company could get bigger and bigger? Just for more money?

The answer and the direction I was searching for came from several sources—my clients, for one. Many of my clients expressed dissatisfaction with their lives. Even though they had enough money to support the lifestyle they had attained, they still had insecurities around money. Their financial wealth often didn't equate to personal happiness. I could relate to their "Is this all there is?" perplexity.

I had a compulsion to learn about how people achieved a financially abundant and happy life. I began to search out and study people who were highly successful in fields I was interested in: finance, business, psychology, and yes, entertainment, too. I discovered common people who had done uncommon things. Whether it be Warren Buffet, Brené Brown, Tony Robbins, or Jennifer Lopez, each of these financially successful people was also making the world a better, healthier, happier, more educated place.

I began to ask myself questions: What do I really value? What do I believe about success, money, achievement, purpose, and what our society needs? What are the strengths I have that I could use to educate, help, and lift others so that they are empowered to build their worth and wealth? I know I exude emotions of joy, fun, love, gratitude, and excitement while needing to calm my impatience and impulsivity. I have a passion for contributing to the happiness of others, happiness that I believe can only come from self-awareness, from personal, spiritual, intellectual, emotional, and financial growth. I want to help people gain worth and wealth from living lives they have designed and implemented, lives that reflect their very best selves.

In addition to my clients and the successful role models I sought out, I also turned to my God. Prayer is talking with God. I prayed. Meditation means quieting our minds and being open to direction and counsel from God. I meditated. I talked. I listened. Very often as I worked, creative thoughts, ideas, and guidance came to me. Prayers were answered.

I believe I am being led toward my life's purpose, which is to use all my knowledge, experience, strengths, and passions to come alongside and help all the other people who are seeking more. Yes, I mean more money, but also more fulfillment, more joy, and more peace. It may sound hokey, but I truly want to be all that I can be so that I can help others to be all that they can be. We must be, ask, listen, and take action to find our true purpose.

If you are truly in search of purpose, I believe yours will unfold for you also through actively reading and responding to the words and exercises I am putting before you. As you define and live your values, beliefs, strengths, and passions, I believe your purpose will emerge as mine has. I will not ask you to write your purpose down in "ink" at this point in your growth process. I do suggest that you write down in "pencil" words, phrases, and sentences that lunge at you as hints of your purpose. Don't stress. Don't labor. Don't evaluate. Just freely and spontaneously rain some random thoughts down right now, right here.

## Action Step—My Purpose

_____

_____

_____

_____

_____

_____

**Own your worth. Find clarity and purpose in your life.**

# CHAPTER 2

# A New Mindset

I believe we are completely responsible for every aspect of our lives. We are free to choose the thoughts we want to hold in our conscious minds. There are many aspects of life over which we do not have control (genetics, our history, others' beliefs and opinions, etc.), but we can definitely control our own thinking and our choices. In order to have an abundance of worth and wealth, you need to live with a wealth and worth mindset.

I think we can agree that all of us make a voluminous number of decisions each day, from very simple to extremely complex ones. Each and every one of those decisions carries with it consequences that we may or may not like, and these decisions often lead to either short- or long-term pain or gain. Though I certainly am not always successful, I strive to make decisions with long-term gain, although unfortunately that often means first experiencing short-term pain.

Here's one of my real-life examples: Eating a handful of potato chips daily offers me pleasure in the short run but total pain when I step on the scale at the end of the month. Whereas daily exercise can be a painful activity in the short run, the long-term gain can lead to a proud, smiling face looking back at me in the full-length mirror. In the realm of money, it may be a downer initially to forgo a luxurious vacation, but down the road there will be great pride in seeing that amount of money compound through investing. Delayed gratification can lead to extended gratification!

Realistically, most of us won't look at every decision from a long-term gain perspective. We owe ourselves some grace and flexibility. However, when faced with any decision that concerns our core values, we better aim for long-term gain about 90 percent of the time. Believe me, I have conversations with myself on a regular basis about my choices and decisions. I'm definitely going for "long-term gain." It has become crystal clear to me that it is our thoughts that lead to the decisions we make and the behaviors we exhibit in our day-to-day lives.

Some of our thoughts we are consciously aware of, while others hang around in our subconscious without our giving them any consideration. We don't recognize their impact on our attitudes and behaviors. We may not realize that there is a need to change or reset our thinking, to interrupt the loop of negative thoughts that we have collected over the years. You know the loop I mean—it's that voice in your head that plays over and over, the one that is filled with "can'ts," "musts," and "should-haves," which have been programmed by us and others based on past experiences. And, in this regard, I doubt there are many topics in life that provoke more thoughts influenced by our past than money and finances.

We all pick up our very first beliefs about money from our family of origin. We learn the uses of money, the power of money, how to make money, who has money, and who doesn't. We get our first experiences with earning, spending, saving, and giving in our youth. Most likely we would be able to identify our parents' values from the way we see them spend their money.

If you experience negative thoughts that regularly infiltrate your mind in an endless loop, you may want to ask yourself if your parents' values are still managing you. Maybe, like your mother did, you find yourself wondering what the neighbors will think. Maybe, like your father did, you quickly respond, "That's too expensive" to your kids when they ask for something.

Are you ready for a different loop, an updated one, a positive one, a personalized one, one that will take you in a different direction? It is time to rethink past beliefs and establish your own fresh ones. Begin to create new goals. Drop any reactive behavior and make rational decisions about future actions according to the values and beliefs you have now established. It's almost magical, the weight that is lifted when you believe you are enough, that you do have what it takes.

When you have firmly decided what is really important, you begin to formulate your plans for growing your worth and wealth. You become focused and energized. There is a lot of insight, plus confidence and power, that comes from owning and understanding your past and how it has constructed and instructed the person you are today. Most exciting of all is that you can do a mindset makeover whenever you choose. And I'd like to point out the added bonus: this makeover is free!

Life will often give you clues as to when some rethinking may be warranted. You know the expression "so-and-so pushed my buttons." I'm guessing that sometime in your life you had your "buttons pushed." All of us can hold repressed feelings, hidden memories, habits, thoughts, desires, and reactions in our subconscious and then, suddenly, something we see, hear, or experience propels them out of the subconscious, right into our conscious mind and into our awareness.

Here's a simple example: You see a large pot of colorful pansies that triggers a memory of your Aunt Penny who loved pansies, had cookies and milk ready every time you visited her, and gave you a generous gift of money as a high school graduation gift. What a sweet memory. You may even find yourself at a nursery in search of some pansies for your patio and later at your desk writing a check out for a niece's special accomplishment.

Here's another example: You have just started to give your two middle schoolers their own allowances. As you begin to explain the parameters of this responsibility, the voice of your father pops into your mind, yelling at the twelve-year-old you for "wasting your money on that garbage." With his disappointed voice also comes your feelings of fear and resentment. Do you repeat history and firmly warn your child not to make "stupid purchases"? Instead, do you consciously, calmly explain that "receiving an allowance allows you kids to learn about how to make choices about your money, and how to live with the consequences of your spending"? Emotional reactions that come from within are signals to scrutinize past messaging and decide how you wish to proceed in light of those messages.

It takes practice to recognize when the patterns, habits, and influences of our past either creep or explode into our consciousness and affect our thoughts and behaviors in the present. It takes even more practice to choose how we want to act considering these blasts from the past. For the purposes of owning our own worth, we need to make sure that our conscious mind needs to be the "controller" that keeps our subconscious mind "controlled." We get to choose our thoughts and our behaviors that result from them. We get to choose our mindset.

## MAKE CERTAIN THOUGHTS AUTOMATIC

When it comes to building financial worth and wealth, we need to focus on and repeat the thoughts and emotions that we have determined will lead us to our desired results. When done repeatedly, our thoughts take on a power that enables, even drives, our behaviors to change. We form new habits. We determine our mindset. This happens only through repeated messages to ourselves, uttered with emotion and put on "automatic."

This kind of automation works by continually conditioning your mind with repeated positive messages or affirmations. I know we have all laughed at memes where a person is looking at themselves in the mirror saying, "You are beautiful and smart. I love you." We can laugh, but automation works. Depending upon childhood experiences or more recent ones, some people have negative thoughts about their worth. Others have positive ones. And, as we have determined, those thoughts often correspond to emotions and behaviors, many of which have become habitual. Automation can work in a positive way or a negative one.

In previous exercises in this book, you have determined your values, beliefs, strengths, and passions. You have been in the process of determining your mindset. Based on personal experience, I can guarantee you that going forward, it is essential to address the negative messages that will haunt you as you choose to make changes in your life.

Acknowledge these negative messages. But be sure to change them. Then watch and see how your life improves.

## Action Step—Thinking over My Thoughts

Okay, I'll start.

In the past I, Dawn, told myself money is limited. There is never enough to support everything I want to do and it's really hard to get more money.

Once I began to confront this negative thought, I realized it came from my past. Though my parents worked extremely hard, I often witnessed conversations expressing their fear of running out of money or heard them make life-impacting decisions, most decisions really, according to "What will it cost?" That made me believe money is limited.

I now believe money can be abundant if and when I challenge and direct my thinking. I always have ways to create wealth if I do so according to my worth. I repeat this affirmation on a daily basis. It has become an automatic positive thought for me.

Your turn . . .

In the past I, _____, told myself this negative thought about money: _____

_____

_____

Once I began to confront this negative thought, I realized it came from my past, from believing _____

_____

_____

_____

I now believe _____

_____

_____

_____

Your assignment: Repeat this positive affirmation daily. It will become an automatic positive thought for you, just as it has for me and many of my clients.

Remember, your life is constantly evolving. Instead of focusing on regrets, celebrate any makeover, reset, or change you choose to make. It's all a part of your journey, even if it is scary to take that first step.

## Zero in on Fear

And since I used the word "scary," let's address the subject of fear. Fear is a strong, distressing human emotion. It comes alive when our values, beliefs, strengths, safety, and security are threatened. Fear can still exist whether such threats are real or imagined. Your fears can really get in the way of you making changes in your life. Like I said before, getting out of your "comfort zone" can be extremely UNcomfortable, mostly because of fear. Believe me, I know fear.

### DAWN'S STORY—FACING MY FEAR

I would say throughout my life I allowed the emotion of fear to dominate my decision-making. As a child I feared not being liked by others. Hearing my parents argue often, there was the constant fear that my family would fall apart. After my parents divorced, I feared being unable to keep relationships with my father and my mother.

When I became an adult, my fears centered around keeping up with friends and advancing my career. I was afraid I wouldn't be able to balance being the breadwinner while also mothering two young girls (eighteen months apart). As if this wasn't enough, additional worries came from owning a financial planning business in an industry dominated by males who were very different from me.

I described myself as "fearfully driven." Fear controlled my life. It wasn't until my move from Minnesota to Arizona that I finally became aware of how deeply fear had a hold on my life. I made a conscious decision to change that. Fear was no longer going to rule my life.

It was the summer of 2017. My husband and I took a trip to Arizona to investigate if we could potentially buy a second home somewhere warm. We chose August because we knew that was one of the hottest months in Arizona. We wanted to see if we could handle the heat. Within days our consensus was "Yep, we can handle this dry heat (as opposed to months-long Minnesota humidity)."

We began to think beyond buying a second home and living there full time. As we spent days getting familiar with the Scottsdale

*continued*

area, we fell in love with it. Scottsdale represents a lifestyle of wellness in terms of being able to live both indoors and outdoors year round thanks to abundant sunshine. Additionally, we found lots of healthy eating options, all the offerings of a big city, and a beautifully landscaped living environment.

As attractive as the Phoenix metro area was and as much as my husband Gary and I could see ourselves living in Arizona, I began to think of all the reasons why we wouldn't be able to make such a move a reality. At that time, we had two teenage daughters who I would never in a million years force to move across the country. The timing could potentially be on our side, I realized, as the girls were in the process of switching schools. Plus, they had both just quit dance, an activity they had been involved in for ten years. There was a lot to think about.

We flew home after that trip and my husband's tentative question echoed in my mind. "That trip was all a dream, wasn't it?" I replied regretfully, "Yeah, I think so." We did have many family conversations about the opportunity, but I kept going back to the fact that there was no way I could continue to run my business in Minnesota and live in Arizona.

Six months later our family decided to spend Christmas in Arizona. We made this decision because I was having a significant conflict with my mother about her drinking and anticipated that staying home in Minnesota seemed destined to be stressful. So, the four of us and the two dogs flew to Arizona for the holidays. Our girls fell in love with the area, especially because the weather was fantastic—sunny and in the '80s. We told the girls we would consider having a second home in this area. Surprisingly, in unison they said, "Let's just move here!" They seemed more enthusiastic and eager than their mama was. I absolutely loved the area but was adamant that I would not be able to keep my business while living in Arizona.

My husband finally said, "Dawn, why would you not be able to live in Arizona? You could just fly back to Minnesota regularly to see your clients, following the same monthly schedule you already have set up for seeing clients." Emotion erupted. "Are you freaking kidding me? I am not getting on a plane every month and flying back to Minnesota. And what are my clients going to say? I don't want them to think that I'm leaving them. This business is my life, and I can't give it up."

My husband countered far more calmly. "Dawn, you do not have to give it up; you can have the best of both worlds if you just stop being so emotional and think it through."

I forced myself to listen. I contemplated the possibility. My conscious mind considered the possibilities while my subconscious spoke by way of shaky hands and gut-wrenching fear. Rationally, I could agree that Gary was right. Client meetings could be conducted in four days each month. My business partner in Minnesota agreed with Gary that we could carry on our business regardless of my change of address.

The nerves continued firing, however, as I admitted, "There's no way I'm going to fly every single month to Minnesota." Over the next couple of weeks, I started to dig deep and realized that my fear of flying was more negatively impacting this decision than adapting to a different way of doing business. I calculated that flying once a month to Minnesota would drop my hours of commuting to and from my home in the suburbs to downtown Minneapolis by 70 percent!

So, I questioned my thinking. "Was I really going to allow an irrational fear of flying get in the way of a move that could be very beneficial for me, my family, and my business?" Clearly, I answered with an emphatic "NO." I decided I was now in charge of my fear, and I was going to learn everything I could about my fear of flying in order to take away its power over me.

In the process I learned that fear can be a good thing. Fear is innate for the purpose of keeping us alive, protecting ourselves from harm. However, fear is not good when it becomes irrational and obsessive, as was my fear of flying. Fear causes anxiety. Anxiety is unhealthy. Fear strips away one's true self, one's potential, one's true worth.

It didn't happen in a day or a month, but with frequent self-talk and prayer, over time I rid myself of the fear and anxiety of flying. I

*continued*

still can't say I like it, but there is no anxiety as I anticipate my next flight or step onto that plane. Conquering, no, maybe it would be more accurate to say managing, my fear of flying convinced me that no longer would I allow fears to determine my decisions. I am in charge of my thoughts. I control them; I'm not going to let them control me or my future.

All four of us love living in Arizona. My family and my business are thriving. My relationships with my clients are every bit as strong as they were when I lived in Minnesota. I have added clients in Arizona. I am living in true worth and wealth.

**Like all emotions, fear needs to be managed.**

I hope you agree, after hearing my story, that fear needs to be managed. Instead of letting your fears stop you, let them motivate you to address them, and then take charge of them and experience the joy of living with less anxiety.

## PUT FEAR TO WORK FOR YOU

I'll give you a couple of examples to explain how this skill can work for you.

| Consideration: What will happen if I quit my job so I can go back to school? | |
| --- | --- |
| Fear | Fear Managed |
| Will I really be able to get a better job after I spend time and money on school? | By going back to school, I will broaden and increase my skills and be better qualified for advancement. |

| Consideration: What if I want to start my own business instead of working for this company? | |
|---|---|
| **Fear** | **Fear Managed** |
| What if I fail? | I have been working for this company for ten years now. I have learned the business. I've been promoted. I have vision of the changes I'd like to make if it was my own. |
| What if my husband doesn't support my decision? | My husband has often heard my thoughts, agreed with them, and supported my goals. |

Fears that are not dealt with can be very debilitating. They can suffocate positive thoughts and actions. They can lead to the use of unhealthy coping skills like overeating and drinking too much. Depression, anxiety, lack of self-confidence, and low self-esteem can follow. Fears stifle the best of who we can be.

Forming a new mindset indicates that talking back to constraining fears allows you to go forward. And, with each success comes increased self-confidence that you can manage fear the next time it creeps into your thinking. When you learn how to take control of your fears, your fears can motivate you to make changes. When you develop a healthy relationship with fear and uncertainty, fear can be the finger pointing toward everything in need of healing in your life.

Let's practice some fear management.

## Action Steps—Facing Fears

Identify your fears. Be sure to check whether they are hiding under the guise of hate, anger, jealousy, pride, or any other emotion. Write down your fears. Be as specific as you possibly can. Believe me, it takes courage not only to explore awareness of them but then to write them down, to own them.

I'm afraid

_____

_____

_____

_____

Don't stop now! Instead, throw some "sass" at those fears. Counter them with "I can do" statements. Write them here.

In spite of my fear, I can _____

_____

_____

_____

Read these "I can do" statements aloud. Feel your shoulders pulling back. Feel your head rising higher. Display these personal positive affirmations where you can read them repeatedly.

We're not done with fear yet. Consider some specific challenges in the following charts. The first gives an example of a challenge—needing to fulfill a requirement before moving forward in your job. Write down the fear that challenge would likely make you feel, and then counter it with a "fear managed" statement.

| Consideration: The job I want to apply for would require me to conduct some training sessions for my employees. | |
|---|---|
| **Fear** | **Fear Managed** |
| I've always been terrified to speak in front of people. | Wait a minute! What I would be talking about is what I've been doing for the past ten years.<br><br>New employees need to know what I know. |

| I get anxious even at the thought of speaking in front of people. | My audience won't be high school freshmen waiting for me to mess up. These people want this information, and the focus should be on the content delivered to them, not on me. |
|---|---|

Now create your own challenge and note the fear and the management that you could bring to the issue to turn it around—with confidence and sass.

| Consideration: | |
|---|---|
| **Fear** | **Fear Managed** |
| | |

| Consideration: | |
|---|---|
| **Fear** | **Fear Managed** |
| | |

Having a conversation like the above with yourself conquers your "What if" fears. Thinking rationally as a skilled, experienced adult will give way to higher energy, positive beliefs, and the "can do" spirit of self-confidence. Increasing the frequency of self-validating statements will allow you to open yourself up to various opportunities. Why waste your energy dwelling on fearful "What ifs" that limit your thinking, undermine your confidence, and hinder your personal growth? No way—not if it's worth and wealth you are after.

## PRACTICE POSITIVITY

When it comes to a person's outlook, I don't think it takes long to determine whether someone is a "half-full" or "half-empty" kind of person. Some people exude positivity. They speak about the good things happening in their lives, and even if they are dealing with a challenging situation at the time, they'll often add, "Yeah, but it could be a lot worse," and continue explaining aspects for which they are grateful.

Others deal with things in an opposite way. Even when they are explaining a benign, or even pleasant circumstance, they'll add, "Yeah, the food was good, but the service was lousy," "Yeah, I got a raise, but the company could have given me a lot more," or "True, we stayed in a beautiful resort in Hawaii and saw spectacular sights, but there were too many people, the price of food was a rip-off, and we had a couple of rainy days when we couldn't do anything."

Of course, I believe in "keeping it real" and sharing the negatives as well as the positives when appropriate, but as much as possible, I think we are all better off trying to find the positive in every situation and being grateful for all that is good in our lives.

For me and many others I know, being positive fills us with energy and desire not only to look for more positives, but to make positives happen for ourselves and others around us. In contrast, focusing on negatives brings me down, stifles my energy level, and robs me of commitment to take action. I don't want those depressing thoughts and feelings to permeate my thinking, affect my decisions, or impact others for any length of time.

Of course, I'm human. I have down days. We all do. I sometimes share painful experiences and feelings with those close to me, but I sure don't want to send the general public an invitation to my "pity party." I don't want negativity to become a habit.

The more you think positively, the more positive things occur in your life. In reality, they may have been occurring all along, but you "see" them when you commit to looking for them. You begin to see the glass half-full, not half-empty. Then, the more positive situations occur in your life, the stronger your belief in positivity.

**Negativity can become a habit.**
**Positivity can become a habit. Choose positivity!**

I'm a strong believer in the empowering aspect of positive thinking. I am secure in my core values, I know my strongest beliefs, I proudly build on my strengths and vow to work on any weaknesses that hamper my worth. I attempt to control my emotions, delight in my passions, and am excited as my purpose reveals itself.

I think right here and right now is the perfect place for us to write down some positive statements about our worth.

Me first . . .

- I have been blessed with abilities and talents that I will use to expand my wealth and that of others. I love being happy and making others happy.

- I am so proud of my efforts to reach out to my readers and others to help them increase self-esteem, security, worth, and wealth.

- Knowing what I know now, looking back, I would definitely have made some different decisions, but I only look back as a source of gaining information to use in moving forward toward more accomplishments in the future.

- I am relieved and excited that I have conquered my fear of flying. (Well, pretty much anyway!)
- I thank God for too many blessings to list.

Your turn to write down some positive statements about your worth:
I am _____

_____

_____

_____

_____

In summary, I believe that focusing on the positives about you and your life puts you in an excellent position for action, for making things happen in your life, for setting your goals. To really work for you, your mindset needs to include an action plan, and that means establishing short- and long-term goals.

## SET GOALS

Let's start this section with visualizing. For some people, visualizing may look a lot like daydreaming, fantasizing, or engaging in make-believe. But that's not at all what visualizing is like for those of us who are making an effort to establish an updated, realistic mindset of wealth and worth. For us, visualizing means conjuring up a plausible picture of what our future could look like, both personally and professionally.

I'll break this down for you. First, take time to visualize your future. Close your eyes and imagine the life you truly desire. Create a clear, mental picture of what you want to do and have. This portrait will reflect your values, beliefs, strengths, emotions, and purpose in action. Did you know that your subconscious mind cannot tell the difference between real experience and one that you imagine? Add passion to what you desire; this channeled, intense emotion can drive your actions in a positive direction.

What do you see when you imagine your future? How about when you add in your superpowers, your passions, and your core values?

Visualization, with positive emotion, has worked for me many times throughout my life. Visualizing the execution of a winning triple jump resulted in me taking a state championship title for track back to my high school. Visualizing my successful work with clients allowed me to become the second most productive financial advisor in the country during my first year in the business. Visualizing led to the purchase of our first brand-new home within seven months of becoming an advisor.

In each case, I conjured up a picture of exactly what I wanted to happen. I pictured myself hitting the jump board, thrusting myself forward, landing in the sand—and standing on the platform having the ribbon with a gold medallion placed around my neck. I "saw" me sitting with clients, poring over their financial information, and creating a financial plan on the computer that showed them how they could grow their money. I visualized their bank accounts—and mine. I had already driven around numerous neighborhoods, toured open houses, and paged through many magazines, and I could picture our new home inside and out. In my mind, the home was mostly decorated before we moved in. "See" yourself doing and living the job and lifestyle to which you aspire.

As you vividly envision the you of your future, you can begin to set goals. You know what a goal is. It's something you want to achieve, a result you are looking for; it's what you are aiming for. Goals are big—and small. Achieving small goals should take you in the direction of your larger goals, if they are clear and specific. Your goals, when linked together one by one, will lead you down the path of designing your ideal life. That's how goals work. You set large, long-term goals (your destination), and then figure out all the small goals (the paths, streets, highways, and interstates) that will take you to your big destination. If goals are to work, you must commit to them. And when you commit to them, you create your life.

**You are the author; you get to write your future.**

Setting goals requires making changes. In turn, making changes requires the setting of goals. A specific, action-oriented plan must be established so that the setting of goals and the making of changes, and vice versa, work together. This presents a challenge to so many people who do not like change. They become reliant on the comfort of repetition, habits, and patterns. Whenever they attempt to do anything new or different, their bodies can react emotionally and physically to fears, stress, and tension. Change can be scary and intimidating.

Even those who proclaim, "I like change," can falter. Their stress also comes from failing to have a plan for making changes and setting goals. Without specifying and prioritizing their goals, they may try to make too many changes at the same time. It's still easy, even for change lovers, to get overwhelmed to the point that they can't implement any one change.

For all of us, if any of our "resistance to change" emotions—like fear of failure, confusion, and impulsivity—are not rationally contradicted with a positive, "I can do" mindset, we can quickly throw "change" out the window, and revert back to "what we've always done." Since making changes is a struggle for many of us, it is vital to create a plan for making change. The old saying is true: "If you always do what you've always done, you'll always get what you've always got."

We've established the important truth that setting goals requires making changes, and making changes necessitates goal setting. Now we need to create our step-by-step action plan. It is essential to establish short-term goals, specifying the small steps, the small changes, that will be needed to reach that long-term goal. The success that is experienced with the attainment of each small goal, each doable change, increases the likelihood of achieving the next small goal, and eventually your larger, long-term goal. Whether you relish change or not, if you want to increase your worth and wealth, you must change in order to meet your goals. So, embrace change, no matter how small—or monumental—those changes are. Get excited about where your goals and changes will take you.

Since you are still reading this book, you definitely do not want "what you've always got." At this point in your journey, tunnel vision can be a good thing. Laser into your short-term goals until they are accomplished, one at a time. You celebrate every single one of them—briefly, and then energetically move on to the next, all in pursuit of those bigger goals for your future.

It is common for people to distinguish their goals as either personal or professional. I propose that you will find that making a change professionally usually requires some adjustments in your personal life and vice versa. When it comes to operating from a beliefs and values perspective, it is nearly impossible, and I believe undesirable, to treat these two areas of your life separately. What you are going for is integration and alignment in the "whole" of your life.

In my early years of being a financial advisor, I found myself balking at my initial training, which focused only on a client's financial wealth. The temptation was to see clients not as unique individuals, but as bank accounts and portfolios. No surprise that when I found the Behavior Financial Advice program, Think2Perform, I zeroed in on their "holistic approach that strengthens the advisor-client relationship."[7] You bet I signed up.

Let's be real; most of us have self-esteem issues, fearful thinking, and

---

7    Lennick, Doug, "Think2Perform," 2013.

other insecurities that follow us around throughout our lives and distract us from our goals, small and large. It's important for you to concentrate (use that laser vision) on what's ahead and think about not only how you want to change and grow, but how you can prepare yourself for the transitions and challenges that you will face in the process.

Change in each of our lives is inevitable, but how you experience and respond to it is in your hands, actually in your mind. I encourage you to reflect on the following thoughts and use them to create your list of personal and professional goals.

## Action Steps—Set Goals

- Make your goals your own.

  - Just because someone else has thought a different way, accomplished something a different way, or lived a different way doesn't mean that you must follow their path. They aren't you! Remember, you already own you. Now, own your goals.

- Be specific.

  - Your goals need to be stated in specifics, with absolute clarity. Spell them out in detail. Write them in the present tense. For example, not "I want to buy a new house." Instead, "I am going to talk to a financial advisor, find out the amount of money I can spend on a home considering my financial means, how much of a down payment I would need to make, and what monthly payments I can afford. With this information in hand, I'll start looking at homes." Staying in this vein, you may then go on to a second goal: "I will be living in a new home within the next twenty-four months. This home has four bedrooms and will be within ten minutes' driving time of my children's school, and the total cost will not exceed 35 percent of my real net income."

Your turn. List three or four goals here. Write down the long-term goal followed by three or four "steps," smaller goals that will take you to the large goal.

Long-term Goal: _____

_____

Short-term Goals: _____

_____

Long-term Goal: _____

_____

Short-term Goals: _____

_____

Long-term Goal: _____

_____

Short-term Goals: _____

_____

Long-term Goal: _____

_____

Short-term Goals: _____

_____

- Keep your goals in sight.
  - Keep your list of long- and short-term goals where you can see them regularly—in your planner, on the bathroom mirror, or as the desktop background of your computer. The forward step to achieving your goals is to revisit them daily. Shut

your eyes and emotionally experience the accomplishment of reaching each of your goals. Do this as if you have already been successful. In other words, visualize! In case you are wondering if visualizing ever felt like silly daydreaming to me, like a waste of time? Definitely. Did I have down, discouraging days? Of course. In fact, I cried multiple times in the early days of becoming an advisor, wanting to quit twice. Instead, I kept telling myself, "Keep the vision, Girl, and don't judge this new opportunity for the first six months." I worked hard and studied my business, kept seeking clients, offered them my enthusiasm and knowledge. My practice grew. Visualization helped assure my "dreams" came true.

- Check your goals for alignment.

  – Read over the goal(s) you have written. It's time to ask yourself an essential question. Remember those five top values you identified a while back? Put those in front of you. Take each goal and examine it. Will you be able to pursue and achieve this goal while upholding the values that you deemed vital to your happiness, to being true to yourself? If not, this goal is not in alignment with what you say is most important to you. Back to the drawing board for you! You didn't think this goal-setting process was going to be easy, did you?

  – To repeat, one thing that is constant in life is change. Our lives are being transformed every day, whether we want it or not. Therefore, we either choose our own paths, the direction in which we wish to grow, or we tumble along without plan or purpose. So take charge. Own everything about you. Own your goals. Commit to your goals. Own your success. Commit to your success.

**ONE WAY TO APPROACH "VISUALIZATION"**

If you are a person who needs your visualization to be very detailed, try this:

· Gather pictures from magazines or take photos and create a vision board of what you want your life to look like—your work life and your home life.

· Place your vision board in a place where you'll see it often and will be reminded of what you are working toward.

· You can even make a virtual vision board; make it the desktop background on your computer.

You will be shocked when you look back at your vision board and see how life unfolded for you, one goal, one achievement, at a time. For me and for you, too, visualization of our specific goals, plus plenty of persistence in pursuing them, will result in our achieving them.

The magic is in taking consistent action! Consistent behavior compounds just like success and money do.

## ACHIEVE THOSE GOALS—SUCCESS COMPOUNDS

What do I mean by "success compounds"? I'm sure you know about earning compound interest on your money. You put money into a savings account at a specific interest rate. At the end of a designated time period, you will see that your account total has grown. Your next application of interest will be on your original investment plus your interest earnings. Your original investment plus your earnings continue to compound again and again. You earn money off the money you just earned. This continues. Your money grows. Your wealth grows!

Achieving a goal is like earning interest. Reach one of your goals and your confidence, motivation, and enthusiasm grow as you achieve the next one and the next one and the next one. As your goals are achieved, your worth grows. Be consistent and persistent. Achieve your goals; grow your worth!

**Consistent positive behavior leads to success, and success compounds.**

## BUILD A SUPPORT SYSTEM

A reality in attaining goals is that no one succeeds alone. You will need to surround yourself with the right people—experts in the fields in which you aren't an expert, supportive people, encouraging people.

We are highly influenced by other humans and their determination of what is "success" or "failure." Be cognizant of who you choose to listen to and spend your time with, let alone who you choose to spend your life with! Likewise, be aware of the environment (which includes people, places, attitudes, and behaviors) in which you operate daily. As you begin to set your goals, make sure you are in an environment conducive to change, inspiration, individuality, and positivity.

If there is any person you know, personally or professionally, who has or does something you're interested in, something you want, seek them out. People love to talk about themselves and their successes, and we can learn from them. People love to help.

Read, study, talk, analyze, dream, borrow, try out, adopt, and adapt. I maintain that the magic to achieving goals is almost 100 percent mindset. Once you have the right mindset and learn how other successful people think, you will be empowered to take action to make your goals a reality.

## CHAPTER 3

# Learning and Letting Go

You have been working very hard on bringing yourself up to date by identifying your current values, beliefs, strengths, and emotions, and you've started formulating your life's purpose. I hope you are feeling a fresh pride in updating all that you are plus feeling an excitement for putting the new you into action.

That action will express itself through your pursuit of the short- and long-term goals you have set, the small and large steps you want to take into your future. I know you know that your action plans will require change. Remember what they say: "If you always do what you've always done, you'll always get what you've always got."

I know you don't want that. You realize you want to do some things differently. You are ready for "new and improved." You want more for yourself and your future, more worth and more wealth.

I have gone through this self-discovery process myself over the years. I've written down my new, more realistic goals. However, a real challenge for me has been letting go of any aspects of my past that either just don't fit me anymore or have become a barrier to my aspirations for my future. I have had to get rid of feelings of regret and guilt, as I mentioned in chapter one about falling out with my former BFF, Kendra. I have, and still am, ridding myself of ineffective, even detrimental habits—practices in conflict with my values. I have laid to rest decisions that turned out to be unproductive, even harmful, and goals that were met but did not deliver the results I had hoped for.

To regret is to feel sorrow or remorse for a situation, for something we did or didn't do or possibly even feel at fault or responsible for. Regret often carries with it some degree of loss, maybe of a relationship, of an opportunity, of time. Guilt often involves committing some kind of offense, against another person or against one's own values and morals. Like with regret, there can be a feeling of responsibility or remorse for some wrong one committed, whether real or perceived.

Regrets and guilt can greatly interfere with, even prevent us from, making changes that we sincerely want to make. To wallow in regret or guilt is a total waste of your emotional energy and precious time. One thing we certainly cannot change is what happened in the past. I believe that regrets and guilt should only be accepted as signals that we have learned from situations we do not intend to repeat. Once we have learned life's lessons, we must let go of the past.

Live. Learn. Let Go. Move On. Repeat as necessary.

**Regrets and guilt should only be accepted as signals that we have learned from situations we do not intend to repeat.**

## DAWN'S STORY—SOPHIE SPEAKS

One day, my thirteen-year-old Sophie walked resolutely into my office while I was working. As I looked up at her, she asked, "Why do you work so much?"

Without giving her question a thought, I automatically responded, "Sophie, I have to work. I have to make money."

Her retort came quickly. "Mom, but why do you work such long hours?"

The thoughts that next flew through my brain and out my mouth were an impatient repeat. "I just told you I need to work so we can afford to do things in life." And in a flash, I heard these same words as an echo, only they were coming out of the mouth of my mother to her preteen daughter—me. I barely noticed Sophie slip out of my office as I remembered how, when I was a little girl, my mother worked Monday and Thursday evenings until 8:00 p.m. Back then, I sat at the front window of our home, waiting to see the headlights of her car pull up into the neighborhood. Many times she was very late, and I sat there for what seemed to be hours waiting for her to get home—to pay attention to me.

So, I asked myself, "Am I really working because I need the money?" I was probably even shaking my head from side to side as I mentally acknowledged an answer. "No, I don't need more money." This realization took my breath away. "Am I really repeating my mother's behaviors?"

Yes, I was. I was working long hours because I loved my work, but also because my work continued to feed my need to be "worthy."

I admitted I had been defining myself as the productive leader at work. Having clients "need" me for financial advice made me feel successful and important. The trust and love I received from my clients allowed me to feel good in my own skin. Though I believe it's a very good thing to find true joy in connecting with and helping others, I had to be honest with myself as I peeled back the truth. Success was filling me up every bit as much as my advice was benefiting my clients. You may ask, "So what's the problem here? You and your clients were both winning!"

*continued*

With a stab to my heart and a tear down my cheek, I lamented, "Sophie isn't winning. She's hurting." I remembered the feeling vividly. So, did I really need to be putting in so many hours? Was I selfishly building my ego at the expense of my relationship with my two daughters?

That caught my attention. I conceded that I was modeling the same behaviors and characteristics that had bothered me so much about my own mother. Regrets and guilt flooded over me. During my growing-up years, I believed it was just money that my mom lacked. But it wasn't money—it was self-worth.

After a good cry followed by sharing time and hugs with Sophie, I promised to myself that I would re-evaluate my work schedule in terms of my core values of building relationships and achieving balance in family life and work. Obviously, change was needed; action was required.

Numerous conversations ensued with my daughters and husband, focusing on their thoughts on this subject of my hours of work. Though a little tough to swallow, I learned that my husband and two teenagers were not wanting to spend hours and hours more with me each week, and they certainly did not want to give up the lifestyle benefits of my career. What it came down to was that they all really wanted to be assured that they were still more important to me than my work. They wanted to know that if they really needed me to be there for them, I would be.

It really came down to improving each of our family members' communication of his/her needs. We had all made lots of assumptions about one another's priorities that needed to be cleared up. Immersing myself in guilt and regret certainly would not have led to these positive results.

## MOVING IN DIFFERENT DIRECTIONS

People change—or don't. In either case, relationships between those individuals change. If two people choose to work amicably and flexibly through changes brought on by life's circumstances, those bonds may be lifelong. More commonly, changes lead to individuals going in different directions, abruptly or gradually. The challenge is to recognize when a relationship is no longer functioning in a healthy manner and either needs to be fixed or ended.

My personal opinion (and experience—I started dating my husband, Gary, at sixteen!) is that when two people, be they spouses, family members, relatives, or friends, both put their relationship as a top priority, then their love and a willingness to communicate openly and honestly will lead to bonding. Each individual then feels valued and enriched.

Essential to such success is a commitment to shared values and pursuit of a win-win outcome in any discussion, decision, or disagreement. Without such a pledge, the relationship will probably dissolve—and probably should. Unhealthy relationships are painful and stressful. They certainly can interfere with the pursuit of any individual's health and happiness as well as their goals toward building worth and wealth. An effective relationship allows each individual to be the best of who they can be.

## DAWN'S STORY–I DO NOT DESERVE THIS

As I've noted previously, working in the financial industry can be intimidating for a woman. In one of my positions in the past, I often felt emotionally threatened. Whether in a team meeting or a one-on-one conference with a colleague, I felt either inadequate or bullied. It's not that anyone with whom I worked literally came out and said, "Dawn, you are unworthy of our firm; you don't live up to our standards." Instead, that message seemed to be implied by how we did business.

When I asked a question or stated an opinion on any topic in a group setting, I felt blown off, dismissed by the shake of the head of one coworker, the rolling of eyes from another. The conversation moved on as if I had said nothing. One time I was confronted

*continued*

condescendingly with, "Dawn, I can't believe you told the client you liked her outfit." The laugh that followed was on the order of "You run like a girl."

One particular day my colleague arrogantly reported, "Dawn, nobody in the office likes you. We've had six people come in and complain about how difficult you are to work with."

When I heard that, I almost passed out. I again took the bully's bait and blurted, "Who said that?" Before the words were even out of my mouth, I knew there would not be an answer.

I also knew my question gave validation to this comment when I really did not believe for a moment that it was true. Yes, I'd been frustrated by assistants who refused to finish tasks I asked them to do while they fell all over themselves to finish the same tasks for my counterparts.

But the reality was, more often than I wished to admit, I left work feeling angry, sad, depressed, resentful, and frustrated. This was surprising, given that I had been recruited to join this company with these words: "It will be such a boost to our business to have a high-performing advisor join us." What had gone wrong?

So for several years I did my job as if I was on probation, paying close attention to all my interactions with the individuals in our office. I worked long and hard to advise clients. I helped them grow their portfolios. I knew I worked with my clients differently, less formally, with a focus on the whole person rather than zeroing in on their bank accounts. I received many referrals. My expertise and style were working. I was making money—for my clients, myself, and my firm. I gained confidence and asserted my opinions. Yet while I gained the respect of several colleagues, there was still that one who seemed more intent on establishing his superiority and "keeping me in my place."

After years with the firm, I ran out of patience with this critical, limiting attitude and atmosphere. I could proudly look at myself in the mirror and proclaim, "I am good at what I do, and I want to keep doing it. I want to be part of a high-performing team. I want to learn and grow in expertise and pass my knowledge on to my clients, even to receptive colleagues. And, I also want to learn from and with all my associates. I want to be a leader in my field, an 'expert.' And yes, I want to make more money."

I found it sad and frustrating that after many years, I saw no opportunity to grow in this current situation. So I made a decision. Enough. Done. I had a right, as does every worker, to be treated in a respectful manner. Working successfully with clients had given me confidence and security; I genuinely believed that I had earned a voice at this corporate table. Because that wasn't happening and I saw no indication that a change of attitude toward me was forthcoming, I left.

If I had had any doubts about my decision, they were erased as I went through the unnecessarily contentious process of ending my association with this organization. Every attempt was made to make me feel guilty. Threats were uttered that I would regret leaving. These behaviors and actions solidified my decision to do so. As a result, a seed of an idea was beginning to grow. How could I create a better working environment more aligned with me?

The stories I share in this book discuss emotional pain. And yes, looking back, I sometimes chide myself for letting each of these situations go on for too long. I could dwell on regret and guilt for not dealing with them more quickly or in a different way. I could hold on to anger, resentment, and sadness. My internal debate continued. How would carrying such emotional baggage benefit me?

Though often painful, I learned so much from every experience I've shared. I learned about myself, my values, and my beliefs. I learned that I have the strengths that work well in my field and with my clients. I learned that some people are not secure enough within themselves to congratulate and fully capitalize on the successes of others. I resolved never to be that kind of leader.

I learned that some people are not team players. I acknowledged my desire to be a leader with the understanding that I cannot succeed in that capacity if I do not have the respect and assistance of a team who I in turn respect, rely upon, and reward. I vowed to be sensitive to the needs of the people I love the most, my family and my dearest friends, while also remaining true to my own needs and values.

Please, don't think for a minute that I live out all these declarations twenty-four seven. I'm human. I screw up at times and have to review and recommit to my goals, check myself on some weaknesses, and resolve to practice attitudes, beliefs, and behaviors that I know work for me.

Now I want to turn the focus to what works for you. What are your stories from the past that have been painful for you? Bringing them to the forefront of your mind and analyzing them will lead to increased emotional health as you shed any residual feelings that you no longer believe are valid or helpful. Once intense emotions are discarded, you will allow yourself rational thought. You will search for your lessons learned. You will be able to center your attention on your rediscovered worth, on your commitment to change, on your present and future as you let go of any aspects of your past that could interfere with pursuing the you that you visualize.

## Action Steps—Growth Opportunities

For your personal growth, answer the following questions as honestly as you can. For some individuals, these answers come as a result of one's own reflection. Others will choose to sort their feelings and thoughts out through discussions with a trusted family member or friend, or even a counselor. Do whatever works for you. Just get going!

What is one of my regrets and/or sources of guilt that I have held on to over the years?

_____

_____

_____

_____

_____

_____

_____

How has this emotional baggage affected my life?

_____

_____

_____

_____

_____

How would it help me to let go of that baggage?

_____

_____

_____

_____

How will I go about this "letting go" process?

_____

_____

_____

_____

_____

_____

What benefits do I visualize for myself once I "let go"?

_____

_____

_____

_____

_____

_____

Own your worth with these words: "This is who I am; this is what I can do." These words proudly announce your fresh mindset. Just to remind you, this isn't bravado. No, this is a legitimate pronouncement you have made. You've worked long and hard to get to this point—to analyze, identify, and define all that is you as a unique human at this moment in your life.

You have selected your core values, updated your beliefs, focused on your strengths, appreciated the importance of managing your emotions, including your fears, and are in the process of articulating your purpose.

You have set goals. You've let go of the past. Congratulations! You have arrived; you have owned your own worth.

All of these achievements are a big deal. Now let's turn from *Own Your Worth* to *Part Two—Earn It!*

# Earn Your Wealth

**You are ready to implement change because: You have owned it!**

✓ Your beliefs are clarified.

✓ Your values are prioritized.

✓ Your strengths have been highlighted.

✓ Your emotions have been acknowledged.

✓ Your rational mind is in charge.

✓ Your goals, small and large, short- and long-term, have been written.

✓ Your interfering baggage has been shed.

**You have done the work! You are ready to move on.**

## CHAPTER 4

# Choosing the Right Career

**M**ost people earn the bulk of their income from the occupation they are in currently. If you enjoy your position, anticipate a promotion, and feel certain that this career path will lead you to an abundant life in every way, then I'm truly happy for you. Feel free to skip this chapter and move on to the next.

But if you find yourself yearning for something else, this chapter is for you. I believe it takes time, and perhaps guidance, to discover your perfect fit. You need to utilize a career selection process that includes analysis of your likes, abilities, strengths, and values, as well as research into which occupations match and reward those very same traits.

My stepmom is a great example of matching traits to an occupation. She loved attending school and "playing school" as a child. She wanted to be a teacher and went on to a fulfilling thirty-four-year career in education, first as a teacher at various grade levels and then as a school counselor.

She has no regrets about her career choice and maintains that it was the perfect match for her.

However, she told me the story of one of her high school students, Addison, who decided in elementary school that she would become a veterinarian because, as Addison said, "I just love being with animals." As my stepmom worked with this sophomore girl, she questioned that choice of career. The two of them researched the requirements of becoming a vet and the responsibilities of the job. Addison wrinkled her nose at the number of science and math courses she would need to take in high school and college. That was a red flag.

My stepmom suggested Addison job shadow a practicing veterinarian. Following that experience, Addison marched into my stepmom's office and declared, "I am not going to be a vet. I could never do surgery on a dog. That was so gross." You can laugh here at such naiveté. My stepmom thought, "Duh, Addison, what did you think vets do? We researched this."

Instead, several career counseling sessions ensued as they looked for a career much better suited to this girl who loved animals. Sad to say, many of us, like Addison, choose a career path without actually entering into the "real world" of that occupation.

Other people might choose the same career as their parents or other adults they admire, rather than what matches their most authentic self or yearnings. They may choose one out of desire for money, fun, excitement, travel, fame, power, or convenience. They also may choose as a result of influences of media, peers, and others.

Sadly, too many are simply unaware of all the career opportunities available to them. Some people may find that the career that worked very well for them as a young adult becomes less manageable as they add a spouse and children to their lives. That was my experience.

## DAWN'S STORY—CAREER SEARCH

I loved singing, dancing, and entertaining, so majoring in music in college seemed a logical career step. However, after a couple of years of music theory, few opportunities for performance, and no interest in becoming a music educator, I thought, why stay in school? Why not just get into the world of entertainment? I performed on a cruise ship, at a resort, and in an amusement park. Great fun, good money, enlightening experiences—for a young woman in her twenties. This lifestyle, however, was not conducive to marriage, family, a house in the "burbs," and job security. So, back to the university I went for a major I created that incorporated business, music, and theater. After graduation I landed a position in events/sales for a hotel/convention venue. Even though there was more money, more responsibility, and more skills gained, I knew this still was not the ultimate job for me.

A dear friend in the financial world talked with me about opportunities as a financial advisor. He knew I really liked working directly with people. I was intrigued with the teaching, influencing, and earning potential this career offered. Working for large and small financial companies then led to creating my own. I am just so grateful that I have landed in a position where I have been able to make a positive impact on the lives of others, as well as my own.

However, true confessions, I must say that my realization that travel by airplane would not be required of a financial advisor added to that career path's appeal. At the time I had an intense fear of getting on a plane. I've always wondered what my life would have been like had that fear not been a factor in my decision-making. Could I have made a bigger impact helping more people sooner?

Maybe. Maybe not. I believe life takes us on journeys we are meant to take. Without my previous limiting beliefs and fear-based decisions, perhaps today I wouldn't be advising you about how to get the most out of your life, personally and financially. I wouldn't be challenging you to examine any fears or limiting beliefs that may be entering your career decision-making.

As you learn more about yourself, you may conclude that you also need to change careers. Though that may be a scary thought initially, as you desire to be in a work situation more aligned with your beliefs, strengths, goals, and purpose, you may find yourself most eager and motivated to find that right setting for you.

Post-high school I was quite sure I wanted a career in music entertainment. Twelve years later I was working as a financial advisor. Yes, searching for the right career match took some time. It may for you also. I want you to earn your income in a way that brings you personal fulfillment as well as the money to have the lifestyle you want. I want you to feel both worthy and wealthy.

## IS YOUR CURRENT JOB A GOOD FIT FOR YOU?

If you have any doubts, I urge you to review all that you learned about yourself in *Part One—Own It* and determine if you are currently in a position that is a good match for who you are as a person at this time in your life. Clarify your degree of job satisfaction and address aspects of your current employment that are causing you stress.

You may relate to some of the following, to people who feel "stuck" in their careers and who question if they have a realistic opportunity to change:

- "I believe I might have more opportunities in a larger city. However, I have a wife, kids in high school, and own a home. It would be complicated to move my family to another city to take a different job."

- "There is a position I would really like to have. To be qualified for it, I would have to go back to school to gain additional skills. This would cost me time and money. I'm afraid I can't afford either."

- "I really dislike this job I've done for almost twenty years. I'm forty years old now. Am I too old to start over? Can I afford to start over? Can I afford not to? I can't stand the thought of twenty more years of this."

I hear a lot of fear in these remarks and many similar ones I've heard over the years. Again, acknowledge your fears, then take control of them with an emphatic retort, "I'm a capable adult. I need to look at other options, choose one, and make it happen." After all, you have spent a lot of time "owning" you. Believe that when you make decisions based on a vision that aligns with your values and capabilities, you choose possibility over fear, you choose positivity over negativity.

You are in search of a path that supports your life goals and that will not allow fear to sabotage them. Fears most certainly will crop up at times. You're human! Now you know how to talk back to them, to control them. Take action. Work toward your goals. You really are ready to "earn it." Any time you feel your stomach turn at changes you are making, take the big steps described below.

## Go Back to Your Core

Your core values, that is. Review your core values and check for alignment with the work you are currently doing. Not being true to one's core values can be very stressful because you are putting your time and effort into work that conflicts with what is most important to you.

For example, if spending time with family is one of your core values and you're an Uber driver, regional salesperson, or an airline pilot who is often gone day and night, no wonder you are so unhappy. If one of your core values is achievement or initiative and you are working your buns off, and yet you are in a job that rewards neither, you are probably discouraged. If you have discovered that you are a very creative person eager to offer new solutions, to suggest an "out of the box" marketing campaign or an innovative adaptation to a current product and there seems to be no avenue for such pursuits in your conservative workplace, your full potential is being stifled. You must be frustrated!

Some people love the challenge, variety, and energy of working with a classroom of middle school kids and stay in that capacity for their entire careers. (God bless you if you are one of those teachers—considering how my girls acted in middle school!) There are others who, over the years, get worn down by that youthful energy and demand. So, think about it. Being a teacher has required you to learn, plan, organize, teach, create, supervise, evaluate. Corporate sales trainers, managers of departments and businesses, and financial advisors are just a few careers that require those same skills.

Don't sell yourself short; you are a commodity in and of yourself. Review and revise your thinking, then your resume, and put yourself out there for some interviews. You may not be totally qualified for another position more appealing to you, but you can sell yourself in a way that depicts you as an achiever with the right attitude and values who is eager to learn. That's just the kind of employee everyone wants.

The big takeaway here is that you can still use your professional strengths in different industries if you think your current one is not offering you the earning potential you desire to fulfill your core values. Research other industries, looking for those where you can transfer your skills and talents and earn a more lucrative wage. Before you exit your current job, be sure to scope out any opportunities you can find or create that may lead to a salary increase. I believe we are all entrepreneurs at our core, so take time to discover the right setting for your "business," the business that is you as a whole person, a commodity, a resource, a treasure.

## Look at What Is Negotiable

Owners, bosses, and supervisors all greatly value employees with the right attitude and work ethic. If you have been such an employee, don't be afraid to propose changes to your job description. Spend some time contemplating ways you could tailor your job to be more suitable to you.

Perhaps your work schedule is negotiable and different hours of work would allow you to go back for additional school/training that would offer other job opportunities in your existing company or in another one. Perhaps you could propose that some of your responsibilities be shifted to others within your organization so you could be more productive working on tasks more aligned with your skill set. Throw out the idea of gaining an extra week of vacation for taking on and completing a large project your company has been contemplating. The key here is to propose a change that you believe would mutually benefit you and your company.

## Check If Anything Is Missing

If some aspect of your current placement, be it social interaction, challenge, or interest, for example, is lacking, but other aspects are quite fulfilling, perhaps you can accommodate those "wants" through a hobby, a part-time job, or volunteering. There may be other avenues you can pursue to fulfill your needs while still staying with the job you currently have.

Then again, maybe you can't. You spend most of your waking hours at work. If you aren't passionate about your work, aren't fully utilizing your strengths, or aren't fulfilled or challenged, you are wasting your precious life. I'd even say that if you don't love what you are doing at least 70 percent of the time, you may want to investigate other work that may be better aligned with your strengths and values.

Nothing is more unsatisfying than spending that much time doing things you don't love. You're probably not earning your potential either. Is there any wonder you are searching for something more?

## GO BACK TO THE DRAWING BOARD—BRIEFLY

Okay, so what if you have explored all the above and concluded that your present career path just isn't right for you any longer? Unless you are in your last years of work before retirement, making a change may be the healthiest and wisest move for you to make. Chronic stress is bad for your mind and body—and is probably already negatively affecting your loved ones. You are pursuing wealth, right? That, of course, can mean wanting more money, but it can also mean improving health, job satisfaction, relationships, and lifestyle.

Take the "new and now" you and state those core values of yours once again. Yes, then list all your strengths, natural ones plus those you've honed through experience. Don't hesitate to ask yourself, "If I don't put any limiting restrictions on myself, what would I like to do? What do I like to do? What gives me purpose?"

Next, go to the internet or the library and explore careers that interest you and that are looking for you, that want people who have your values, goals, strengths, etc. You might visit the website Careerexplorer.com and take their thirty-minute career test. Afterward, write down three aspects of your job that are a good match for you. Talk with people in the career fields you are exploring, perhaps even do a job shadow the way Addison, the animal lover, did during high school. Step into the shoes of someone in a different career. How do those shoes fit you? In summary, get into the "real world" of that job.

Once you find a match (or several), dig into what it would take to qualify you for that new occupation. Remember, there are grants and loans out there for retraining, as well as certificates and degrees that can be earned online or through part-time attendance at an institution. Every college and university provides career assessments and has counselors to help you answer questions and develop a plan. Job placement specialists and employment specialists are a Google search away.

Within your specific circumstances, decide whether you can prepare for a different career while remaining in your present one, or if in the long run, it would actually pay off to quit now and throw yourself fully into pursuit of a new direction. This would not be an impulsive decision, but one arrived at after honest, diligent self-exploration and goal setting and many a discussion with loved ones affected by your decision and from whom you wish support.

## Action Steps—About My Job

Here's your opportunity to analyze your fit into your current job. I'll guide you from your current job right into "what could be." As you visualize a career more closely aligned with today's you, you will become more motivated. Goal setting gets you working toward those future possibilities. Setting up your support system both encourages you and commits you to following through. You're ready. You're set. So, go!

List the aspects of your job that are a good match for you.

_____

_____

_____

_____

List the aspects that are not a good match for you.

_____

_____

_____

_____

List any aspects of your present position that you would like to negotiate with your employer.

_____

_____

_____

_____

Explain the changes you choose to make in the way you currently earn your income. Be specific and realistic as you add new short- and long-term goals to those you have already formulated previously.

_____

_____

_____

_____

_____

Since you are human, you undoubtedly have fears creeping into your psyche as you contemplate change. Write them down here. Then, with conviction, talk back to them with "I can" and "I will" statements.

_____

_____

_____

_____

_____

_____

List the people from whom you will look for support.

_____

_____

_____

_____

When you truly "own it" your career decisions become more obvious. You have to do what you have to do—for you—now. No apologies or regrets for the past. Relegate those past choices to your "live and learn" history book. Focus on present self-awareness and future potential. Commit to "earn it" by being true to yourself and by living a personal life and a work life in alignment with who you are now and all that is important to you now.

## CHAPTER 5

# Earning the Right Income

Most people probably think that the right income for them would be more income. Examine the features of your current work that are meeting your values and goals and utilizing your abilities and talents. I think you would agree there are more facets to a satisfying job than a paycheck alone. Question if your current income is fair compensation for the work that you do and allows you the standard of living you desire. If the amount of money you are currently making is not enough, you have choices. You either need to figure out how to make more money or how to get more out of the money you have. It's about building purposeful wealth.

Earning an income is the catalyst for experiencing either plenty or scarcity, so it is vitally important you get paid what you are worth. You need to earn enough money not just to meet monthly obligations, but enough to also save and pay taxes *and* have some fun in your life. Despite the size of your income, saving for your future needs to be a nonnegotiable item. A portion of your income must be saved for emergencies as well as to support your future.

**Saving for your future is nonnegotiable.**

Think in terms of continuously growing your skills, knowledge, and experience for advancement purposes. Let your work ethic set you apart from other workers so that your potential becomes obvious and opportunities for promotion come your way. I have witnessed people complain about their low pay, not realizing either how unproductive they really are, or how their attitudes negatively affect supervisors and coworkers. Attitude adjustments are surely within your control.

There may be times while you are working in your current position that it becomes obvious that more education, experience, or personal development are necessary for you to grow into a higher-salaried position. Knowing your worth is understanding your current skill and experiential levels in terms of future opportunities. To earn the most you can earn, you need to acquire a combination of usable skills and positive behaviors. Self-awareness and productivity are keys to salary advancement at any level.

## SALARY NEGOTIATIONS

Here is an observation I have made while working with clients over the years. In general, women don't like to talk about money, and they certainly don't like to ask for money. Women have been entering the workplace and making money in increasing numbers for six or more decades now. Yet, it seems like there are still lingering vestiges of old beliefs that it is primarily men who do and should earn money, invest money, and save money. Women are to spend said money for the needs of husbands, children, and themselves. In the past, money matters were thought to be men's matters. Certainly, such stereotypical behaviors have changed; yet, to a lesser degree, past practices and attitudes persist.

I want to say loud and clear to women: It is not only acceptable for you to talk about money, earn money, spend money, save money, and invest money, but it is also essential for your self-esteem and financial security to understand money, make money, and handle money wisely. You are allowed to want money, to expect more money, to want a big life—if you are willing to work for that money. If your workplace allows for it, you are allowed—and I encourage you—to negotiate your salary. Money does matter to women as well as men.

Money matters to you! You want and need to earn money. You have attained skills and experience. You have made yourself valuable to your place of employment. You like your job and believe it is the right one for you. Such realizations should certainly boost your self-confidence. You may have reached a point where you want and believe you are worthy of a salary increase.

Sometimes, even with self-confidence and belief that you are worth more than you are earning currently, asking for money or benefits from a superior can be very stressful and intimidating. In the early days of my career, I sure felt that way. It certainly became easier to ask, though to be honest, it never became entirely easy. My advice is to take small steps. Begin with investigating.

You must understand how raises and promotions are handled at your workplace. There are some professions, like teaching or policing, or like hourly or union jobs, that simply do not allow for negotiation. My clients who are teachers tell me that when handed their salary chart, they sweep a finger across to the amount of education they have attained, then down to their number of years of experience, and at the intersection lies their salary. Period. No such thing as "negotiation" exists. Therefore, many teachers start early in their careers to take additional courses for credit, working toward their master's degree so they get to the top of that salary schedule as soon as possible.

Other professionals attain more income from adding specific skills and certifications or displaying exemplary performance, work ethic, and attitude. In the business field, several factors may be taken into consideration for establishing one's salary. Be prepared to highlight how you exhibit those traits and behaviors. Keep salary-earning policies in mind throughout your career search, especially if you want to be able to influence the amount of money you will earn.

To keep it real, friends in a variety of fields and settings have told me that sometimes it is quite challenging to discover the basis for salary determination at their companies. Keep your eyes and ears open for information and opportunity. There are also resources online, for example Salary.com, where you can learn more about your income opportunities.

Whether you work for an agency, institution, company, or corporation, give yourself the best opportunity to secure a wage at the top end of the range. It has been my experience that many employers expect you to negotiate. However, one of my clients who has been in human resources for over thirty years told me that in her experience, 70 percent of employees are not earning at the top end of their salary range. If a top-end salary has not been offered to you before you accept the position, try negotiating a sixty- to ninety- to 180-day review. In other words, propose to your boss that if you prove your worth in the above time period, you will be considered for a raise. Remind yourself that you have nothing to lose by eagerly and respectfully asserting yourself toward a higher salary. To expect more, deliver more!

If you are one of the fortunate workers able to negotiate your salary, remember that your negotiating power strengthens from doing the following:

- Research the salary range for the position you hold in your workplace.

- Discover the salary range for comparable positions at other companies in your area.

- Review the skill set you have developed as well as your accomplishments and any awards you have earned.

- Prepare the "sales pitch" of the personal and technical skills you bring to the position and to the company. Ask yourself:

  ✓ How am I creating more value for the company?

  ✓ What makes me indispensable?

  ✓ What new efficiencies am I bringing to my position?

  ✓ What special skills/talents have I brought to my workplace?

  ✓ How do I improve the atmosphere of my work environment?

- Practice aloud a mock negotiating session, and even record it for analysis of your clarity, tone, content, and emotional state. Train yourself to breathe slowly and quietly. This will bring you calm and help you avoid being the first to speak during awkward silences. (I believe it is better to be uncomfortable for a short time while negotiating than to be financially uncomfortable for the coming year.)

- Keep eye contact while waiting for the negotiator to initiate the process and throughout the session. Feel free to pause before answering questions or making comments, showing that you are determined to make thoughtful, articulate responses.

- Be real. Be honest. Arrive with a mindset of positivity, confidence, willingness to listen, and eagerness to promote yourself.

- Ask provocative questions such as:

  ✓ What productivity level needs to be exhibited in this position for the company to realize that the employee is surpassing expectations and deserves greater compensation?

  ✓ What are the most important tasks that must be completed to make the biggest impact for the company's success?

- Listen to the negotiator's answers to your questions and then seize any opportunity to explain how you are already working at an advanced level and therefore merit a salary at that next level.

- Enthusiastically share your commitment to being an employee of exemplary performance and therefore worthy of top dollar.

- Consider the first offer you are given. However, continue to "sell" yourself if you think the negotiator may be open to a second, higher proposal.

- Think big. Go high. Show that you are comfortable, confident, and prepared to do respectful battle to get what you deserve. With this approach, again, what do you have to lose? Much more important, what do you have to gain?

Negotiating for more money may not be your only desire or option. Perhaps you would like to negotiate your hours of work, coming in earlier so you can leave earlier and be home for your children when they return from school. You may be able to work four ten-hour days as opposed to five eight-hour ones, perhaps saving you a day's worth of childcare. Are there job-sharing opportunities? Investigate the possibility of your company paying for personal and professional development courses that will allow you to earn an advanced degree or certificates which, in turn, will avail you of the opportunity for promotion and more money.

Whatever you can envision that will enhance your job satisfaction with the conditions of your work, create a proposal that will mutually benefit both you and your employer. Again, take time to review, research, prepare, and execute. Outstanding employees are the backbone of any business, company, or institution. They are valued. Employers want to keep them. Be one of those "star performers" and increase your possibilities of negotiation and advancement. Bring your worth to the table to gain more wealth.

## DAWN'S STORY—NEGOTIATING

I acknowledge that I am in a field where salary negotiation is permitted, even expected. I am very grateful for that. I also have become quite assertive as a result of increasing my knowledge, experience, productivity, and income. Over the past twenty years, I have successfully negotiated my salary each time. I have put tens of thousands of dollars into my pocket by doing so. As I recommended to you, prior to my salary negotiation meeting, I researched the range of salaries offered to others of my skill and experience levels and asked for a salary in the top 20 percent of that range. This became my baseline salary.

In addition to this baseline salary requirement, I had other expenses I wanted to have covered, specifically in two areas. The first was household services (like housecleaning, laundry, etc.). These chores sucked way too much time and energy out of my life. If I could afford to hire these out, that would allow me to focus more of my time and energy on my job. I figured this "outsourcing" usually costs between two and five thousand dollars per year. The second was to cover my savings expense of 15 percent of my gross income.

Therefore, when I added the additional income I needed for "outsourcing" and savings expense to my baseline requirement, I now had what I called the target salary I was going for. Throughout the years, when I held strong to my target salary, I got paid exactly what I asked for—even when salary negotiations were tough.

I work in a male-dominated industry where it has been

*continued*

continuously implied that I'm not worth making as much or more than any of my male counterparts. One time I was confronted with a rhetorical question: "Why would you ever need more income?" To me, the implication was that my lifestyle expenses should never exceed a certain amount, as though I should not want more!

This question was asked of me by a male colleague who was making more than double what I was. My interpretation was that I was not to feel worthy of living a more abundant lifestyle. Insulting, especially since I knew that I always delivered more than was expected for my salary.

I experienced several such money manipulation games where it was implied that I had no right to more money, or worse, that I was "overpaid." I was uncomfortable, even angry, in those salary negotiation situations. Still, during the negotiation, I respectfully listened and was silent at times. I kept eye contact and then said, "Well, I hear what you are saying, but I disagree. I always deliver more than my pay requires."

With that, I did receive my target salary. However, when my work environment became such that I was made to feel unworthy of fair pay, felt disrespected, and grew tired of the salary struggle, I made the decision to go elsewhere, and eventually, to start my own company. I developed a clear understanding of my financial worth and decided to accept nothing less.

## PICKING UP A "SIDE HUSTLE"

It is possible, perhaps even common, to love your job and receive pay at the top of the salary range but still need/want more income. If this is true for you, then perhaps it's time for you to get creative with a "side hustle." Now that you know what your "superpowers" are from part one, take your specialized skills and look for places where you could use them yourself or teach them to others. Identify those experiences and the expertise you can share with the world.

If you are hesitant to jump into such an endeavor by yourself, seek others who share your talents or complement them. Work your side hustle as a team. Alone or together, get creative and think outside the box. Figure out what our world needs that you can provide, and go for it. In today's world there are multiple online, income-generating opportunities which could provide a way for you to earn additional income right from the comfort of your home.

For example, let's say your "gifted power" is photography. Take that passion and host an affordable online course for people with an interest in that field. That is the beauty of technology. You could educate others on the technical, sales, and/or marketing aspects of photography. Another possibility would be to focus only on a niche market with certain types of clients who would value working with you under a monthly membership program. This would help you retain clients, give you a reliable monthly income, and make hiring the right photographer easier on the client. Look for other creative ways to earn an income using your superpowers.

Do be aware that starting a business from the ground up will be challenging. It will take time, hard work, consistency, and self-discipline. One of the main reasons start-up businesses aren't successful is because the entrepreneur doesn't know how to market and/or gives up way too soon. Research the opportunities, put together a plan, and act! It can be an exciting way to make extra income if the project properly aligns with you!

## Action Steps—Considering Your Earning Potential

Let's have you personalize this issue of earning more money. Here are some questions to answer that will help you get a better grip on your thoughts about your salary and salary negotiations going forward.

Are you currently earning the right salary for you? Why or why not?

_____

_____

_____

_____

_____

_____

In your occupation, are you able to negotiate a fair salary? Are there "benefits" other than or in addition to a salary increase you would like to pursue? If so, create your "sales pitch."

_____

_____

_____

_____

_____

Are you giving any thought to adding a "side hustle" to your life? Explain some of the possibilities you are considering. (If you choose to go this route, prepare yourself for putting a lot of time and effort into this endeavor, motivating yourself with the belief that your success will enrich your bank account and your lifestyle.)

_____

_____

_____

_____

_____

## CHAPTER 6

# Creating the Right Spending Plan for You

I'm guessing your head might be spinning right now as you assess your career choice, the positive and negative aspects of your current job, the degree of your satisfaction with your salary and lifestyle, and the possibility of making changes. Please don't stress. You have choices. You are not stuck. You have opportunities to consider. You may want to make changes. You may have decisions to make. Those are all good things. Please consider this personal and professional assessment you are making as offering you possibilities, not problems. It's all about your mindset.

At this point in your evaluation of the present you, you may have concluded that you really like your life after all. In looking at the pros and cons of your current job, you may determine that the positives far outweigh the negatives. You might arrive at a place of peace, believing that you do have alignment regarding your values, goals, personality, the position you hold, and the life you lead. Still, I urge you to continue reading as I address financial issues and matters that all of us must deal with, whether or not we feel a current sense of worth and wealth.

Others of you may be a bit overwhelmed because you are still mid-process of "owning it," setting goals, assessing your job and lifestyle satisfaction. I can hear you saying, "Dawn, I have so many thoughts and questions swirling around in my mind right now, and yet you want me now to think about a spending plan? Yikes, no can do."

My advice to you: relax. You have choices here. If you want to continue working on content and action steps in previous chapters, go back and do that. Remember, you didn't get to this place in your life in a day; you aren't going to get where you want to be in a day either. You set the pace, not me or anyone else. Find the way that works best for you.

I have read many self-help books straight through the first time to get "the big picture." Then I went back and slowly "worked" my way through the information and activities in them from beginning to end. Be sure to do whatever works best for you. You are in control of your own walk toward worth and wealth.

## THE IMPORTANCE OF A SPENDING PLAN

The philosophy behind building a wealth plan professes that one's updated beliefs, values, purpose, strengths, and goals should be aligned with his/her current income, assets, and debts, that is, aligned with an individual's total worth. Developing such a plan requires a person, you in this case, to carefully analyze the above and check for compatibility among all aspects of your life and lifestyle.

Few people have actually achieved this ideal status—at least not permanently. I often review my spending plan, looking for places for improvement based on changes in my personal life, in federal and state laws, and in my business. I'm guessing you would welcome guidance, so I'm going to help you create your new, fluid spending plan.

True confessions here. Is it possible that you don't really believe you can do better than you are currently doing? You believe your income is not sufficient for the lifestyle you wish. Why is that? Perhaps you have stayed in a position that does not allow for advancement. Possibly you have not developed the skills that would lead to that promotion and thus elevate your income. Or, like so many, you may have fallen into random spending habits that are neither in accordance with your stated values nor allow for savings or debt reduction.

To help you, I want you to challenge your thinking regarding spending your money. Overspending is a common behavior in our society. Why? In my years of experience advising people, I have found there are two general reasons:

- **People believe they have insufficient worth.** They spend due to this perception of low self-worth and a failure to manage their emotions. Some treat emotional upheavals with impulsive shopping therapy. They allow their spending to be influenced by others, for status, to compete, to cover up for insufficient funds. Possibly based on familial history, some resist any suggestions of budgeting, feeling resistant to control and structure. Compulsive spending can become a dangerous lifestyle. While making decisions about money is not the time to allow emotions to lead. Inevitably this results in poor money decisions. Emotional regulation around our money is key.

- **People believe they have insufficient wealth.** Often this is due to not thinking rationally and not having a spending plan. It is so easy to underestimate the cumulative cost of small and large purchases made regularly without thought. Extensive use of credit cards, carrying over large balances, and either not realizing or not caring about high interest rates can lead to exorbitant debt. Some people accept debt to the point of not attempting to systematically pay down what they owe.

To conclude, many times too many of us spend too much time and money on things in life that provide little or no personal and/or professional value. We do this mainly because we are searching for "something" to bring us happiness, to fill an unmet need. Many times, we spend money on the wrong things. We impulsively buy expensive or even frivolous items because we are happy or depressed, feel insecure and fearful, or "just want it now."

Too often our purchases do not fill our emotional hunger. They provide only short-term pleasure and leave us still "wanting." Such mindless spending sabotages one's attainment of personal and financial worth and wealth. To reverse such unproductive habits, there needs to be a concerted effort to increase usable income, spend thoughtfully and purposely, and commit to reducing debt.

**Live for today but prepare for tomorrow.**

## STRIVE FOR PURPOSEFUL SPENDING

I have no intention of sending you on a guilt trip. If you fully realize that you are purposely ordering that four-dollar beverage, buying that expensive Louis Vuitton bag, ordering new golf clubs, taking a luxury cruise—to celebrate, soothe your hurt feelings, or "just because you can"—then go for it and enjoy. I'd be the last person on this planet to stifle spontaneity or shopping "therapy."

However, the key here is "owning it." You need to have an awareness of and take responsibility for the choices you are making. The danger comes in "finding yourself" sipping a cappuccino, carrying a new purse, swinging your new driver, or cruising to the Caribbean in reaction to unidentified emotions and irrational thinking. Such spending is not purposeful. You also want to question if such emotional spending is rare for you or has become a habit.

So here is a significant point I want you to understand. Focusing on improving decisions that will "move the money needle" is more important than saving a few bucks here and there. I'm talking about earning higher incomes, properly managing debt, and understanding how taxes work. This is where the magic happens. You need to revise your money messages. I want you to get the fancy beverage, handbag, clubs, cruise if that is what you want and it's true to your values (and of course, has been negotiated with your significant other). But here's the catch: I want you to buy for the *right* reasons. Select purchases and experiences that are aligned with your values and stop wasting money on things that do nothing for life fulfillment.

What I do want you to do is spend money that:

- allows you to pursue your core value goals,

- you have already established in your spending plan,

- will enable you to live out what is important to you at home and at work.

In other words, as I said before, spend for the right reasons. Make your money work for you. Use it to buy things, services, and experiences that will take you closer to achieving your core value goals rather than take you off course. This ain't easy! I know that, especially if the people you hang around with do mindless spending and therefore "appear" to be doing better than you are. I told you that achieving your stated goals in life will take self-discipline and focus. Often, it also involves risk-taking. (And facing fears with rational thinking rather than with high-priced shoes! Just sayin'!) Honestly, I prefer that you get to have both—peace of mind *and* great shoes!

You must accept that risk comes with changing jobs, negotiating a higher salary, and taking on debt for training and education. I don't want you to be frugal while pursuing these areas. Instead, do engage in quality spending and making wise choices. I believe you will be willing to take on calculated risk when you have gained self-confidence and pride from successfully establishing and following your chosen highway to your destination, your goals. You will be more comfortable with risk when you "own it," when you realize how much of your life and wealth are clearly under your control as you "earn it."

## THE ESSENTIAL COMPONENTS OF A SPENDING PLAN

It is essential that we first understand all the aspects of our spending that must be covered by the income we earn. As I explain each component, when applicable, I will also offer you figures that I believe take an ordinary plan to one that's "ideal."

> **Earnings/Income**—Now! Today! Your income includes all the monies you have coming into your household through salary and bonuses. This includes any additional income from investments, rental property, inheritance, etc. This is your gross income. The money you bring home after taxes is your net income.

I'd like to say a few words here regarding income that has been inherited. As I said previously, there are significant differences between our grandparents'/parents' generations and ours when it comes to beliefs and behaviors regarding money. We have inherited some of those so must choose those we keep and those we discard. Staying in the same job for thirty years, rather than being a sense of pride, may actually be unwise and unprofitable nowadays. "Pinching pennies" may no longer be necessary. Today there are many more options for saving money than previously. Such ideas and practices may no longer serve us well in today's world. However, I also want to stress that previous generations did a much better job of spending **and** saving money than the general population is doing today.

Our parents and grandparents saved a much higher percentage of their income than we do. They delayed gratification to save and thus create security for themselves. It saddens me that parents and grandparents lived way below their means while now many of us live way above our means. Consequently, it is likely that any money we or our children may inherit from our parents and grandparents will be used to pay off debt or allow us to continue our overspending behaviors. It's so important for the current and younger generations to build their own wealth. Wise use of inherited wealth and continued wealth building of our own are the only ways future generations will be able to survive and thrive.

> **Taxes**—Income taxes are based on the amount of money you earn, or your income. Income includes the money you make at your job, interest you earn on things such as savings accounts and investments, money you earn from rental properties, money you win gambling, money you inherit, and pretty much anything that adds to your financial worth over the course of the year. The tax on this income is the percentage of your income the government takes, both federal and state (and sometimes local). Depending on the state you live in, this income tax can be anywhere

from nothing to over 10 percent of your income. Add this to the up to 30 to 40 percent that the federal government can take. That's a big chunk of your income that goes right to governments.

Based on income, each household falls into a particular tax bracket. A side note here as well as a hint of things to come: in part three, I will be giving you ideas for methods of minimizing your taxes and tax bracket. Still, paying your taxes is not optional!

> **Savings**—You need your money to work as hard for you as you work for it. It's desirable to arrive in the future at a place of financial independence where you no longer need to work for money. For most, we call that place "retirement." To some, however, it may come at an earlier point when they decide to take a "sabbatical" for education, travel, or pursuing a hobby. To others, they strive for a time and place in which they have total control of how they spend their time and money. In all cases, saving for your future is nonnegotiable. I encourage everyone I work with to save no less than 15 percent of their annual gross income. Without doing so, you lose control of your goals, your worth, and your wealth.

Because saving is so key to long-term financial success and security, I'd like to offer a bit more explanation on this topic. Just so we're clear, "gross" income is your income before you pay taxes. Because there are many different tax brackets, the percentage of your gross income that is claimed by taxes varies according to each earner's income. I believe you understand that the higher the tax bracket you are in, the less percentage of your gross income will be available to each of the other areas (core values, household expenses, financial gifts, and debt reduction).

Therefore, when it comes to money available for spending, you must first set aside the percentage you have to allot for taxes in your income bracket, plus 15 percent of your gross income for savings. This is Dawn Dahlby's rule. You get to spend what is left after those percentages are taken out.

**My rule: Every household needs to be saving 15 percent of its gross income no matter its tax bracket.**

When it comes to analyzing your spending, the money left is my financial definition of net income—after taxes and savings.

> **Debt**—Yes, I know, the best debt is no debt. However, let's be realistic. Most people do have debt. I have debt. Most important is the distinction between good debt and bad debt. I personally believe that you should only carry the good kind of debt, which involves taking out loans to pay for an appreciating asset, such as a home. And also, my professional opinion, the good debt should never exceed 35 percent of a person's "real net income" (after taxes and savings). More about this topic is upcoming as you read on.

### DAWN'S STORY—DISASTER TO DEBT

This story is not my own, but that of clients who got themselves into debt and really struggled to get out of their financial hole. This couple owned a home but did not have a cash reserve (a fund of accessible cash) in place. The husband, who was laid off from his

*continued*

job, became extremely fearful that he and his wife would not be able to make their house payment. They reactively put their home up for sale, and in a rush to sell, sold the house at a $30,000 loss.

This couple then decided to buy a smaller home where they thought they would never have to worry about being in such an alarming position again. Two months later the husband was reemployed by the same employer. If only this couple had had a three-month emergency cash fund built up, they would never have lost that $30,000. That $30,000 invested at a 7 percent annualized rate of return could have turned into $32,000. Instead, they had $0. A lack of a cash reserve cost them a sizable chunk of change.

This story gets worse. Prior to this real estate loss, this conscientious couple never had any other debt. This costly experience brought out negative emotions of fear, embarrassment, and unworthiness. Sadly, and ironically, their painful emotions led to a spending frenzy and within twelve months they had racked up over $25,000 of credit card debt. This debt was a combination of some emergency expenses on their recently purchased home, along with some emotional spending.

On top of this, the couple began using another credit card and before long had amassed another $10,000 of debt. One of the credit cards had an interest rate of 16.9 percent and the other 14.5 percent, which resulted in them paying approximately $5400 annually just in interest. They paid $930 per month for these two credit cards for almost five years. Once again, they were back to zero debt.

However, had they taken that $930 each month and invested it at an average rate of return of 7 percent over those five years, they would be seeing an account of $66,500. Due to not having a cash reserve account, in just a five-year period this couple felt forced to sell their home at a loss, then racked up sizable credit card debt, giving up the opportunity to have $98,500 ($32,000 + $66,500). In five years! Think about what that amount could have turned into in another five years when this husband and wife would still have only been in their midforties. Yikes!

**Expenses**—In simplest terms, expenses are the cost of living your life. These are broken down into two categories:

Fixed—These are the expenses you absolutely must pay regularly, such as house and car payments or rent, utility bills, hospital, and dental bills. You may also pay regularly for various insurances, donations to church, education, etc.

Discretionary—This is a very broad category because it includes everything else you choose to spend money on: food (in and out of home), clothing, household furnishings, home and car maintenance, education, recreation and entertainment, fuel, donations, gifts, etc.

Determining which category to put each item in might prove to be an interesting, challenging, and revealing assignment in and of itself. Your spouse may put an annual golf membership into fixed expenses, whereas your fixed expenses may include a twice-monthly manicure/pedicure!

Let's say that, for example, in a conversation with one of your friends, you learned that she considers her gym membership "fixed" while you would place it under a "discretionary" expense. Your retired parents and you may disagree on the proper category for private school, summer camps, and name-brand athletic shoes for your children. Determining expenses as fixed or discretionary is only pertinent to the person or persons sharing an income. I continually refer you to your core values because these should definitely help you clarify whether an expense is essential to your life or up for discussion.

## Spending Plan Recap

Before we get into the details of your expenses, let's recap these components of an ideal spending plan. Start with your gross income, all the earnings you take in in a year. All expenses come out of your gross income. Your annual taxes are determined by the size of that income, and they must be taken out first. I believe the next amount to come out should be 15 percent for savings. I want my clients to think of this slice of their pie as nonnegotiable. (You can see that Dawn's definition of net income is after taxes and savings are taken out.) Take another 35 percent out for debt reduction. In part three, I will go into more detail about the payoff you will receive by adhering to the discipline of paying down your debt wisely.

## Further Breakdown of Spending Plan

Taxes. Savings. Debt reduction. I believe that addressing these three wisely is key to long-term wealth building, so I have put them as top priorities for handling your earned income. So many people don't do this because the following categories of spending may seem like higher priorities in their day-to-day living.

### HOUSEHOLD EXPENSES

It costs money to run a household. Whatever you call home needs fuel, furnishings, cleaning, and maintenance. Your family needs clothes, food, transportation and its fuel, education, recreation, entertainment, etc. In today's world you probably want a variety of modes of communication. Childcare can certainly be an essential but substantial expense. Only you can determine which of these expenses end up being fixed or discretionary. To some degree, this decision also is a matter of values—yours and your family's. In general, I suggest about 35 percent of Dawn's definition of "net" income (the dollars left after taxes and 15 percent savings) should go for these household expenses.

## CORE VALUE EXPENSES

Another 25 percent of this "net" income (again, after taxes and 15 percent savings) should go toward pursuing your core values. In part one, while deciding to "own it," you settled on your top core values. The cost of living out your core values can vary greatly. Some will cost you little. If you desire some luxury in pursuing a particular value, your output of money may be far greater.

Ideally, but also realistically, when you get to your net income after savings, taxes, and paying down any debt you have, you will have only 25 percent of that pot for spending on your core values, of which you have listed five of them. Some of these five may cost you little or nothing. Therefore, you will have to determine if they each get 5 percent of that 25 percent or if you want to prioritize differently and spend only on a couple of your goals to begin with. My point is that in your ideal plan, you still have a finite number of dollars to spend. It will certainly be a thought-provoking process to prioritize how you want to live out your values.

Perhaps the few examples in the following chart will clarify the cost of living your core values:

| Value | Low (or No) Cost Activities | High Cost Activities | Actually Earns $$ |
|---|---|---|---|
| Health | Walking outside daily ($$ on good walking shoes) | Joining a gym ($$ on membership) | Being a fitness instructor (full- or part-time) |
| | Hiking ($$ on hiking shoes, equipment, travel) | "Building" home gym ($$ on construction &/or equipment) | |
| | Taking dietary supplements | | Selling/taking supplements |
| | Preparing healthy food/eating at home | Eating healthy but usually out | |

*continued*

| Value | Low (or No) Cost Activities | High Cost Activities | Actually Earns $$ |
|---|---|---|---|
| Health (cont.) | Purchasing hair/beauty products and services | | Selling/providing products and services |
| Relationships | Playing games with others | Golfing | Working at a career that involves a lot of interaction with others |
| | Phoning/texting others | Coffee/dinners | |
| Ambition | Stellar work ethic | Education/training | Working toward raises/promotions (This could cost you some $$ if extra hours require more childcare, cleaning services/eating out) |
| Adventure | "Staycation" (remaining at home to take advantage of local sights or doing family activities & projects) | All-inclusive Hawaiian resort | Working at a job that involves traveling and/ or working in a variety of settings |
| | Camping | Cruising | |

## Living Your Core Values

I want to emphasize that there are no right or wrong choices here. These are the values you have selected. These are lifestyle activities you deem important to your happiness. Well and good. To keep it real in our financial planning process, it is just vital that you establish the price of living out each value.

This holds true for all your core values. I think the best news is that by going through this process, you will toss out items and activities that you have been spending money on in the past but that, in retrospect, did not give you all that much reward, particularly in the long-term. Check out your fondest memories, the ones that have endured over time. Perhaps there will be some insight here as to not only your core values, but also the cost of those precious moments.

I'd like to add that it feels really good when you have the money to buy whatever it is that you want, but instead, you say "no" to a specific, tempting purchase. That, my friend, is power! If you are out with your friends and one of them decides to buy that expensive whatever, and you say "no" to doing the same, not because you can't afford it, but because you have other priorities, that is living in control! That is living your core values. That is living wealthy.

An additional bonus occurs when you realize that you are living out one or more of your core values while making a living. In other words, you are making more money while living out your values than you are spending on them. To me, this is the ultimate in living my life, of attaining job satisfaction and fulfillment. I consider myself most fortunate to have discovered a career that requires the strengths I have, the skills I have developed, and satisfies my core values. It earns me the money I want and need for the lifestyle I have dreamed of. I am indeed grateful. And, because of that, I still have one other category to fulfill under "expenses."

## CHARITABLE GIVING

I believe in sharing some of what we earn. I quantify "some" as 5 percent of one's NET (my definition of net) earnings. Giving back acknowledges our gratitude for our worth and wealth. "Giving" can take so many forms and is only limited by the imagination of the giver. Traditionally, many people's "giving" encompassed their annual contribution to their church. That may still be one of your chosen charities.

You may select charities that have personal meaning for you, from those that support a specific medical research subject, veterans, survivors of intimate violence, children, pets, the arts, or saving the environment, just to name a very few. There are so, so many organizations that would appreciate your financial support or your time, energy, and skills.

Hiring a babysitter so you can work four hours at the local food pantry can certainly be seen as charitable giving, as can donating to that pantry. Driving to and from your local hospital once a week to volunteer in the surgery waiting room is giving. Sending greeting cards weekly to your great-aunt in a nursing home is charitable. You choose your method(s) of giving and who you would like to be the receiver of your generosity. When you think about it, I believe you would agree that our society wouldn't operate as it does without all the volunteering and contributions made by its citizens.

## PUTTING A WEALTH ALIGNMENT SPENDING PLAN TOGETHER

At this point I'd like to present you with a sample spending plan, then lead you toward analyzing your current actual spending plan. Then, based on your annual gross income, you will create your own ideal spending plan.

For some of us, understanding comes through seeing a concrete example of how a plan can be set up. Adding dollar amounts can increase clarity. To others, numbers can be overwhelming. I certainly don't want to add to your stress and confusion.

Take a look at this sample plan:

### A SAMPLE IDEAL WEALTH ALIGNMENT SPENDING PLAN*

| | |
|---|---|
| Household's Annual Gross Income: | $100,000 |
| Minus Savings (15 percent of gross income) | ($15,000) |

| | |
|---|---|
| Taxable Income Subtotal: | $85,000 |
| Minus Taxes ($100,000 gross income assumes a 24 percent bracket, but instead would be 22 percent because savings was put into qualified retirement plans, making 100 percent of savings tax-deferred and not counted toward taxable income) | ($18,700) |
| Subtotal: | $66,300 |

*For a single individual in 2021, only looking at federal tax brackets (not state tax)

This $66,300 figure is how I define actual net income. This household now has $66,300 of net income for its expenses.

Striving for the "ideal" spending plan, the following components will be addressed as follows:

| | |
|---|---|
| Minus Money for Debt Reduction (35 percent) (Of the Net Income—$66,300) | ($23,205) |
| Subtotal: | $43,095 |

(If you don't have debt to pay down or if your debt load is small, congratulations. Take this extra money and split it between your core values, household expenses, debt reduction, and your financial gifts.)

| | |
|---|---|
| Subtotal: | $43,095 |
| Minus Household Expenses (35 percent of $66,300) | ($23,205) |
| Subtotal: | $19,890 |
| Minus Expenses to Live Core Values (25 percent of $66,300) | ($16,575) |
| Subtotal: | $3,315 |
| Minus Charitable Giving (5 percent of $66,300) | ($3,315) |
| Money Left: | $0,000 |

# EVALUATE YOUR ACTUAL SPENDING

From here I urge you to review the current actual expenditure of your gross income. You have some tough work to do here, so take out your journal (or your iPad), grab a pen (or your power cord) and your beverage of choice, and go to a quiet place without distractions.

The task ahead will take a considerable amount of time and research, but I promise will be super revealing of your current mode of operating with your money. If you have a spouse or significant other with whom you share financial resources, ask, beg, or bribe them to join you in this endeavor. You both have a lot to gain from your joint effort to create your current spending plan. I want you to take all the time you need to think deeply and write down YOUR reality.

. As a wealth advisor, I can't stress enough the importance of having a spending plan. Please don't look at a plan as a "limiting" budget but instead a plan that you control to build your total worth. I promise you that conquering this task will be the foundation of building your wealth. It is your roadmap to achieving both financial freedom and financial security at the same time.

If needed, please refer once again to the sample spending plan I introduced to you. As you begin to fill out the "worksheet" I'm giving you, do not even think about figuring out percentages at this point. Instead, supply a dollar amount for each category. This will be your closest estimate of your current earnings and spending. Though admittedly, dollars and cents add up to tens, hundreds, and thousands of dollars, approximations are most acceptable here. This is for you, remember, not for anybody else.

## Action Steps—My Spending Reality

### MY HOUSEHOLD'S ACTUAL SPENDING PLAN

| | |
|---|---|
| Our household's combined annual Gross Income | $___ |
| Minus Actual Annual Savings | -$___ |
| Subtotal: | $___ |
| Minus Actual Annual Taxes Paid | -$___ |
| Subtotal: | $___ |
| Our actual net income left for Expenses | $___ |
| Debt reduction | -$___ |
| My household now has this amount available as Net Income for our annual Expenses. So, start this Expenses section with this figure. | $___ |
| Minus our current annual household expenses | -$___ |
| Subtotal | $___ |
| Minus expenses for living my/our core values | -$___ |
| Subtotal | $___ |
| Minus our current annual charitable giving | -$___ |
| Total | $___ |

This is what's left! (You could have a figure that is "in the black" [underspending] or "in the red" [overspending].)

## ACTUAL VERSUS IDEAL PERCENTAGES

The next step in this exercise is for you to calculate some percentages. The following chart will give you my suggested ideal percentages to compare to your actual percentages. Starting with your gross income, calculate the percentage of this income that is being taken out for federal and state taxes. Figure out the percentage you are currently saving and what percentage you are paying toward debt reduction. After those three percentages have been listed, what is left is the total percentage you have left for your net income (my definition). So, move on to your overall expenses, determining the percentages of your net income you pay to live out your core values, pay for the operation of your household, and contribute to charitable causes. Put this information in chart form like this:

### What Comes Off of a Household's Gross Income

| Ideal Percentage | My Actual Percentage |
|---|---|
| Taxes (per tax bracket after having deferred some $$ via Savings Plans) | ___ percent (based on my Tax Bracket percent) |
| Savings (15 percent) | ___ percent |
| What Comes Off My Household's Net Income (AFTER Taxes and Savings) | |
| Paying Down Debt (35 percent) | ___ percent |
| Household Expenses (35 percent) | ___ percent |
| Core Value Expenses (25 percent) | ___ percent |
| Charitable Giving (5 percent) | ___ percent |

I hope you will want to do some comparison here between your actual percentages and what I have presented to you as ideal. This should lead to much thinking on your part and/or lots of discussion between you and your partner. What changes will you need and want to make that will get you closer to your ideal spending and savings plan? No panicking is allowed here. Your current situation is what it is. It is a waste of time to wallow in pity and regret over past decisions you can't change. Instead, think positively, "I understand my actual expenditures and I can do something about them. I want to take my life and my finances in a new and improved direction."

Be proud of yourself. You have "owned up" to how your household utilizes the money you earn. Let's take it one step further. I am providing you with still another "worksheet." This time, use the "ideal" percentages I have presented to you to create your ideal spending plan. Considering your annual gross income, calculate the dollars you should be spending on each component of your personal plan.

### My Household's "Ideal" Wealth Alignment Spending Plan

| | |
|---|---|
| Our Household's Combined Annual Gross Income: | $___ |
| Minus Actual Annual Savings (15 percent) | -$___ |
| Subtotal: | $___ |
| Minus actual Annual Taxes Paid | -$___ |
| Subtotal: | $___ |
| My household now has this amount available as Net Income for our annual Expenses. So, start this Expenses section with this figure. | $___ |
| Minus Actual Dollars Spent on Debt Reduction Annually (35 percent) | -$___ |
| Minus Our Current Annual Household Expenses (35 percent) | -$___ |
| Subtotal: | $___ |
| Minus Expenses for Living My/Our Core Values (25 percent) | -$___ |
| Subtotal: | $___ |
| Minus Our Current Annual Charitable Giving (5 percent) | -$___ |
| Total: | $___ |

CONGRATULATIONS! You have accomplished a monumental

task. I hope you feel "in the real world" about your actual spending and saving and that it has become quite clear to you the areas in which you wish to make changes. Compare your actual percentages to the ideal ones. I'm hoping you will experience numerous "aha" moments that clarify for you why growing "wealth" has been problematic for you.

I'm guessing you will find something far different than what you have discovered would be "ideal" in your situation. I bet you may find a lower percentage of savings, a higher percentage of debt, and a feeling that you do not have enough money to fully live out your core values, let alone meet your regular expenses and share with others. How can I make such a prediction? Because this is the most common scenario I see when first working with clients' finances. The good news is that this, then, is their signal, and yours, that changes are needed.

## Overspending? Go Back to Your Core Values

We often spend too much because we are looking for "more." More what? We crave more "life"! If you want more "life," buying more things that don't provide value is the biggest waste of your hard-earned income. Therefore, this is the perfect moment for putting your mental awareness and energy into the solutions to your lack of enough money. Antidotes for overspending are:

1. Learn the power and potential of saving. Remember, saving is nonnegotiable!

2. Earn more income—in alignment with your strengths.

3. Spend in alignment with your values. In other words, prioritize your money.

Commit to one, two, or three of these practices and you will have total wealth; you will be living "in abundance." Logically, the above choices are simple, though not easy. You will either need to pursue a position and/or a side hustle that will allow you to earn a higher income, or you will need to decrease the amount of money you spend.

It's all about analyzing and prioritizing your current core values, modifying your lifestyle to accommodate them, and figuring out if the money you now make is enough or not enough. I promise you, when you do this, you will find a deeper fulfillment in the lifestyle you have created plus clarify your path to greater wealth. You will be able to live for today without sacrificing your tomorrow. Best of all, you will gain confidence in determining your own future and the motivation to meet your short- and long-term goals.

In conclusion, your spending plan, like other self-worth tasks I've put before you, needs to be specific. You are trying to discover the full, realistic cost (the dollars and cents) of your daily living. That you must pay taxes is nonnegotiable. However, as I have shown you earlier in this section, and which I will explore further in part three, there are ways to offset your taxes through wise investment in a variety of savings options.

I believe the amount of your savings should also be nonnegotiable, 15 percent of your gross income. So that your life doesn't become a financial nightmare, your debts need to be addressed. Your values and how you live them are uniquely yours, but in your "ideal" wealth alignment spending plan, spending money targeted toward your core values is nonnegotiable. That's the challenge of truly living your core values.

I have observed that most people are not able to achieve both financial security and spending freedom at the same time. They are either overspending and under-saving, meaning they are spending freely but feel little sense of financial security. Or they are underspending and over-saving. That is, they have focused on attaining financial security but do not feel free to spend their money on what they value and enjoy. There can be many reasons why people struggle greatly with balancing spending and saving. Many have not revisited beliefs about money carried with them from youth. Others try to fill a myriad of emotional needs through either spending or saving. So many lack education and understanding of how money works, living only for the moment, living paycheck to paycheck. You could probably come up with other explanations from your own experience.

When you begin to think about and discuss what adjustments you need and want to make to get you closer to that ideal, to your ideal, you will have made great progress toward living a life of wealth and worth, freedom and security, a life of fulfillment, contentment, and happiness. Isn't this what we are all striving for?

Please be proud that you are in the distinct minority of people who have so specifically itemized where their gross income goes. You also are among the few who can vividly see the areas where your current plan is not working for you. More importantly, you have discovered how to take components of your plan from actual to ideal.

As you worked your way through *Part One—Own It!*, you brought yourself to the point of identifying your up-to-date beliefs, strengths, core values, emotions, goals, and purpose. In this section, *Part Two—Earn It!*, you have reevaluated your current job to see if it is the right one for you or if you need to make changes in the amount and way you earn income. I promise you when you have analyzed your real and realistic spending plan, your path forward to *Part Three—Grow It!* will be so much clearer to you. Your newly discovered insight will allow you to put your precious time and energy into those tasks that will truly enrich your life and that make you wealthy in all senses of the word.

You have reached the point of analyzing and revising your personal spending plan. I believe you are on your way to becoming one of the rare persons intent on achieving both financial security and spending freedom at the same time. I urge you to commit yourself to living out the ideal spending plan you have created. It works. I promise you it works—if you work at it.

## CHAPTER 7

# Understanding How Debt Occurs

Yes, I know, the best debt is no debt. However, let's be realistic. The majority of people do have debt. I have debt. Most important is the distinction between good debt and bad debt. I personally believe that you should only carry the good kind of debt, which involves taking out loans to pay for an appreciating asset, like a house.

Does this paragraph sound familiar to you? I hope so. You read it earlier. Debt is such an important topic; repetition is warranted. When discussing their financial status with any of my clients, you can bet that this topic comes up consistently. So often, when you mention debt, the first question that comes from people is "How much money do I owe?" Having debt involves so much more than just buying things you can't pay for at the time. That's way too simple of an explanation for a complicated process that is as much or more about thoughts, emotions, and habits as it is about math.

# AN ACCEPTABLE AMOUNT OF DEBT

There are so many differences of opinion regarding how much debt one should have. Some experts say zero; others say no more than 36 percent of your gross income should be committed to any type of debt. As an experienced CFP® who has witnessed many clients' financial success as well as their spending behaviors, I personally believe total debt payments should not exceed 35 percent of anyone's "real net income" (after taxes and 15 percent savings).

I also believe that in an ideal world, the only debt one should have is house (real estate) debt. As a realist, I understand that many people also need to take out auto loans or lease cars, which would also require payments. Let me go on record with the assertion that automobile loans are never "good" loans, even when offered at 0 percent interest, because automobiles are a depreciating asset. The best way to pay for a car would be to pay cash, unless the cash is earning a rate of return above the interest cost of the car! However, studies have shown that only 8-12 percent of the population pay cash for their cars. People have car payments.

These payments of buying or leasing a car along with a mortgage payment should not exceed 35 percent of an individual's/family's net (after taxes and savings) household income. The reason I recommend total debt of no more than 35 percent is because I understand human spending behavior in our instant gratification world. It is so easy to go into debt. Again, being a realist, my message to you isn't about eliminating all debt and thus not having a life today. No, it's about aligning wealth and living wisely today in order to have enough money to live in freedom and security tomorrow.

When I have worked with clients whose debt has increased beyond 35 percent of "real net income," I have witnessed the beginning of real financial distress. The mortgage lender may have told them, "Yes, you qualify for this house because your total debt doesn't exceed 36 percent of your gross income." Well, I'm here to tell you, don't fall for that. In my educated and experienced mind, with debt of 36 percent of your gross income, you do not qualify for that mortgage. That lender is doing you a disservice. That is just too much overall debt, which can grow even larger when a household is then unable to pay for daily living expenses.

Time and time again I have worked with people who live in houses they can't afford, dine out regularly, shop for luxury brands, go to concerts, travel, etc. These lifestyle activities and possessions fight for your dollars. Remember, they are your dollars, and you rationally need to determine whether adding debt by making such purchases is in your financial best interest. Most likely, it is not!

## GOOD DEBT VERSUS BAD DEBT

You need to learn about good debt (warning: there's not a lot to learn on this topic) and break free from bad debt (warning: there's a lot to learn here). You need to determine if the spending in your life is appropriate, planned, controlled, and fulfilling, or if it is haphazard, impulsive, and unsatisfying long-term.

Studying these topics will probably also bring to light many facets, sometimes conflicting, of your relationship with money. If you find there's nothing left at the end of the month, you aren't alone. A Pew Research Center study found that "just 46 percent of Americans earn more than they spend every month."[8] Less than half!

Drilling down into the details reveals a bad situation. "Members of Generation X—which includes people ages 40-55—have the highest

---

8    Danielle Bautista and Tim Ranzetta, "Question of the Day: What percent of Americans spend more than they earn?," *NGPF Blog*, February 26, 2018, https://www.ngpf.org/blog/budgeting/question-of-the-day-what-percent-of-americans-spend-more-than-they-earn/.

debt of any generation, carrying an average credit card balance of $7,155, according to Experian data from Q3 2020."[9] That's too much!

Even worse, through my experience I have found that when people only pay the minimum on their credit card balance, they end up paying more than double for whatever they purchased. In this case, that would be over $15,000. Does that take your breath away like it does mine?

## EMOTIONAL RESPONSES TO UNDERLYING DEBT

Commitment to debt reduction comes through learning about how we think, learning how to manage our emotions, getting direction from experts, and planning how to deal with our unique financial situation. When you are in the middle of making decisions about money, don't let emotions overpower rational thought. Allowing this will most likely result in poor money-making decisions. Emotional regulation around our money is vital. This means being mindful when making any kinds of purchases, large and small. Many times, we are unaware of how our continued spending behaviors, rooted in our emotions, start to add up and too often end up on credit cards.

Emotions from our past experiences can impact our current spending behaviors. Current emotions, for example, being upset due to conflicts arising at work or in our family, can negatively impact our spending behaviors today. Can we "justify" spending a few bucks here and there (called retail therapy) when we are experiencing negative emotion? Yes, of course we can!

Occasionally, when life doesn't go our way, go buy those (non-designer . . . wink wink) shoes, get those little extra things that make you feel better in the moment. Shop guilt-free and enjoy them. We all do this. It's a part of life. Just be sure this isn't happening weekly (or monthly), and

9    Stefan Lembo Stolba, "How Many People Have Credit Card Debt?," *Experian* (blog), December 16, 2020, https://www.experian.com/blogs/ask-experian/how-many-people-have-credit-card-debt/.

that you are willing to give up another buying or investing opportunity in return for this retail therapy expenditure. It's about prioritizing our spending and being aware of our spending habits.

Be starkly aware of how often you find yourself making emotional purchases. Make sure this kind of spending doesn't become a repeatable behavior that could lead you into frivolous debt that has now cost you double, if not triple (thanks to interest rates), for that thing that really only made you "happy" for a few hours.

Personal awareness comes from understanding how our emotions tie into our overall lifestyle spending. We must know what the underlying reasons are for why we spend like we do. The goal is to challenge our purchases, big and small, and make sure most, if not all of them, are aligned with our values and our long-term financial vision, and not fueled by past or present emotions.

## Emotions That Cause Us to Overspend

What are the underlying emotions to our overspending? I have typically found we overspend due to an unmet emotional need from the past. We may have grown up with some unhealed hardships not even related to money, but now we spend too much money on a lavish lifestyle because it makes us feel vindicated, in control, important, and worthy. Emotions and money choices are about understanding the reasons behind our spending decisions.

If these spending decisions are in alignment with our values, beliefs, and income *and* they provide emotional fulfillment, then our relationship with money is a sound one. However, if we are overspending money for any other reason than alignment with our purposes, our past relationship with money should be examined. So many people I have worked with realized that when they healed from their past, they made better money decisions and, in turn, gained more security and freedom, which are core human needs.

As we discuss concealed emotions, I also want you to be aware of your thinking and how you talk to yourself about money. Are you constantly talking about how everything is expensive? ("I can't afford that.") Are you always putting negative energy around the cost of everything in your life? ("I hate having to spend so much on childcare.") You may even feel that you are not deserving of more money. You may have a negative relationship with money and not even be aware of it.

Do you associate money with power, greed, or selfishness? If so, you may believe that if you have a lot of money, you are power-hungry, greedy, and selfish. Where did those beliefs come from? These and other reactions to money may stem from teachings, hardships, and/or conflicts experienced in your past. When not acknowledged and dealt with, such "baggage" may trigger irrational spending or hesitation in spending even for sensible wants and needs. Most of the hardships we have in life continue to be larger than what they truly are because of our unmanaged emotions, fearful thinking, and limiting beliefs.

Typically, when we have issues in life, it's because our emotions are out of alignment with our core values. Dealing with emotional dilemmas is a signpost of values conflicts—a signal that changes are needed in our thinking and behavior. It's human to be emotional, to experience a myriad of emotions for a multitude of reasons. However, to be a person of worth and wealth, we must recognize and manage such emotions. We must not allow them to negatively impact our decision-making skills and, thus, our life and lifestyle.

## REPLACING REACTION WITH REASON

One way to manage our emotions is to have a plan in place for when our emotions get the best of us. Such turmoil often happens when we experience negative emotions resulting from differing opinions and perspectives from others we care about. Emotional upheaval also often occurs when our bank account gives us the reality check that our financial situation is not what we think it is or should be. It certainly isn't what we want it to be.

All these scenarios can lead to panic. No sound and reasonable thinking and decision-making occurs when a person is in panic mode. You need a plan to halt or reverse "going down the rabbit hole" into either an emotionally driven spending spree or a debilitating depression.

Make a conscious decision of how you are going to handle your next issue around money. First, become aware of the emotions you are experiencing. You may be shocked at how much negative energy arises within when the topic of money comes up. If you are experiencing anger, peel back the many reasons why you are angry. Keep peeling until you get to the basis of your emotion.

I bet you have already experienced being in an intense emotional state. You absolutely cannot think clearly. Interrupt the progression. If another person is involved in your money frustration, think about asking the other person to give you some time to take a break. Try taking some deep breaths, going for a walk, working out, or even taking time for some meditation.

Try sorting out your thoughts and feelings on paper so you can read and think about them and revise them as needed. Do whatever works to calm yourself down, giving yourself time to talk down overt anger, fear, or whatever emotion has control of you. Through planning and practicing this rational process, you become more resilient and stronger. You are also doing the other person a favor by allowing each of you time to cool down, think reasonably, and present thoughts to one another in a calm, more businesslike manner. Words won't get said that can't be taken back. Prepare in order to attack the problem, not one another.

Over time, you are teaching yourself a new pattern of dealing with intense emotions. Having this self-discipline will build your sense of control and in turn, your self-esteem and your self-confidence.

**Exercise control over your emotions, engage in rational thinking, and choose to act rather than react.**

My job as a wealth advisor is to teach my clients this process of managing their emotions and decision-making regarding their spending and saving behaviors. Our decisions give birth to our behaviors, which direct our lives. It's those internal decisions that really matter. Our external lives are a result of our internal decisions. Make them wisely.

Emotions and money have a strong relationship with one another. An easy way to remember how to manage your emotions, especially when making a financial decision, is to use the "ABCDE" Method.

> Awareness—What is your current emotional state? What caused it?
> Beliefs—What do you believe about this situation? Is it true?
> Core Values—Is this financial decision in alignment with your core values?
> Decision—Make your decision based on rational thinking.
> Emotions—Manage your emotions. Control them; don't let them control you!

Going through this process gives you enough time to pause and breathe so you can think logically and act rationally. Spending in general, and taking on debt specifically, need to be the result of careful decisions made after a realistic analysis of your needs and core values.

## CHAPTER 8

# The Right Way to Manage Debt

Other than maybe some retired people, almost everyone has some amount of debt. Few of us can pay cash for our homes and cars. My philosophy is that it is wisest to minimize debt by spending your money only on those goods and services that are aligned with your values and, as previously discussed, fall within the 25 percent of your real net income.

If living your values costs money, I believe you should be spending your money on those values rather than focusing only on paying down debt. If it is extremely important to you to own a home, unless you win a lottery or inherit wealth, you will be taking on debt. And yes, you are right. Over time this strategy will cost you more money, but the goal is to Live WELLthy™, enjoying life's experiences today *and* tomorrow.

However, as I stated in the very beginning of this book, true wealth is not limited to how much money you earn or spend. Living WELLthy™ involves increasing your self-worth and your income simultaneously. It involves spending your time and your financial resources in alignment with what you maintain you need for happiness, freedom, and security.

## ACHIEVING A POSITIVE GAIN POSITION

If you are the type of person who wants your debts gone, please be aggressive and make that happen. I suggest not doubling up on your mortgage payments, however. Instead, take that extra cash and create a "mortgage payback account." Instead of making that double mortgage payment, take half that money and invest it. The purpose of doing this is to earn more in interest on your investment than you would gain by making that double payment. For example, if your mortgage is costing you 3.5 percent annually and your "mortgage payback account," your investment, is earning 6 percent, the difference of 2.5 percent is extra money that you wouldn't have by just putting it on your mortgage. In other words, put your money where it can make the most money for you. Investments will not always net a 6 percent, 7 percent, or 8 percent on that money, but over time, your account should average that range of return if you are a moderate to aggressive investor.

This proposed return of 6 percent or more would be based on the time frame and risk you are willing to take on. The longer time you have, the more risk you can take, the higher potential rate of return. Regardless, any return over 3.5 percent in this example (or even any return over 3.5 percent minus your potential tax write-off on your mortgage) puts you in a positive gain position even after paying the tax on these earnings.

Granted, some experts would urge you to just pay down the mortgage debt. However, I believe if you are the type of person that is disciplined to get rid of debt ASAP, then you are also disciplined to save the difference between your actual mortgage payment and the extra cash you have to invest. The key here is to diversify your extra savings and understand the calculated risks you are taking on with this strategy. (I'll be addressing this topic in part three.)

I have seen this strategy work for many of my clients. Over time I have witnessed clients taking an extra $700 and instead of applying it to their mortgage, they invest it, receiving a net 2.5 percent return. Over the next fifteen years they have an additional $152,686. That is some real extra cash! Also, we all know real estate doesn't always appreciate during the time we live in our primary residence, so putting this extra cash into an investment account provides more diversification and flexibility when looking at one's comprehensive financial plan.

## CREDIT CARD CALAMITY

In dealing with spending and debt, too many people look to the use of credit cards as a way to "have their cake and eat it, too." I have heard: "Here's my solution. I will just charge this one concert ticket on my card and then pay it off." That's a reasonable intention until a friend calls and extends an invitation to happy hour and dinner. That bill gets put on the card. Another friend calls days later with an offer to accompany her on an "inexpensive" trip that really didn't end up being inexpensive at all. It gets put on the card. Next, a car breaks down and requires immediate repair. It, too, gets put on the card.

The "solution" to "just charge the concert" quickly turns into $5,000 of debt on a credit card at 16.9 percent interest. This amount, then, can't be paid off all at one time. That $5,000 easily becomes $5,845 even without adding any more charges. Though everyone likes the freedom of buying what they want when they want it, if you want to see your money grow, curb impulsive spending and minimize the use of credit cards. Both will reduce your stress in the long run.

No matter how you look at it, credit card debt is a killer. Never does having a credit card balance make financial sense. I know that so many of us use plastic to pay for most everything. Unless you are 100 percent committed to paying off every dime of credit card balance every single month, use a debit card. Since there is a limited amount of money in your checking account, when there is no balance, there will be no purchase allowed. I repeat, never allow there to be a balance on your credit card statement. And if there is currently, this is a financial issue that needs to be addressed immediately.

Many people believe that you need a credit card to build credit. While successful use of a credit card can help raise your credit score, the most important factors are establishing a history of on-time payments to all creditors and keeping debt low in relation to the amount of credit available to you. You need a history of paying all your bills on time, including student loans, rent payments, mortgage payments, car payments, etc. You do not need a credit card to build credit. There are too many risky behavior issues that take the lead, so too often having access to a credit card to build credit isn't worth the additional behavioral risk it comes with.

This credit card warning applies to all of us. Please don't think I'm just talking to you. I have been in a situation with credit card debt and so have many of my clients, friends, and family. That is why I can speak firsthand how horrible it is to keep a credit card balance. Some of my clients didn't nip their credit card debt in the bud. They didn't have a disciplined plan to pay off the debt nor the intention to get rid of those cards and their associated risk immediately. These were the clients who continued to have debt issues for years.

## DAWN'S STORY—FROM PURCHASES TO PANIC

Let me give you an example of a client who came to me with $25,000 of credit card debt. Before addressing the "how" to come up with a plan to pay this debt off, I needed to address the "why" she had such debt in the first place. I said, "Tell me about how you came to have $25,000 of debt on these three credit cards." I discovered that most times, it was due to her need for instant gratification. She and her husband wanted that particular vacation now. They deserved it, right? After the expensive Caribbean vacation, there was a broken washer/dryer, then some unforeseen medical bills, a puppy their kids just had to have, plus swimming lessons she wanted for her children.

She was overwhelmed to the point of panic.

Helping her and her husband out of their predicament involved quite a painful process. Eventually, they were able to see that 80 percent of their debt was accumulated from spending money on activities and stuff that wasn't related to their core values. They finally admitted to numerous unpaid purchases that provided minimal value in their lives and gave them little or no long-term benefit. Yes, she owned up to spending more money than they had at the time. That's the bottom line.

To put this in dollars and cents (using debt payment calculations from https://undebt.it), 80 percent of the $25,000 was spent on things and activities this couple did not define as core values. That is $20,000. The interest rate on this "wasteful debt" was 19.6 percent, or approximately $3,920 for the year. This $3,920 in interest could have almost paid for the "necessary" expense of $5,000, and this couple would have had zero credit card debt.

Instead, they were paying the minimum payments, which would then take them twenty-four years to pay off. This debt led to an interest accumulation of approximately $46,858. If they had taken that $20,000 spent on unnecessary expenses and invested it at 7 percent over the twenty-four years, they would have had approximately $106,788! So, after twenty-four years, they paid out $46,858 when they could have bankrolled $106,788. Hard to believe until you see it in print.

Had this couple realized initially that they had the choice of a debt of $46,858 or a nest egg of $106,788, they most certainly would never have gone the route they did.

In summary, when using credit cards, there is a terrible price to pay for carrying balances over and being charged interest every month. When making a credit card purchase, remind yourself that you must pay for the item as soon as the bill comes. If you can't do that, reconsider the purchase. Trust me, you'll be so happy you did. No one wants to pay double for any purchase they make.

This real-life example illustrates what I mean about making smart decisions with your money, decisions which put you in control, give you power, and make you money. Large and even small purchases can add up quickly. Spending via credit cards can become a mindless habit. I am quite emphatic when I tell you that you can't allow yourself to have credit card debt. Period! If you currently have credit card debt, reach out to an expert to help you. Put the nail in the coffin of that debt because there is a way out—a calculated way without shame or guilt.

Here is one of my favorite websites to show you a plan to pay down your debt in an effective way: https://undebt.it.[10] You can input your debts and the software will show you a few different ways to implement a payment plan. If you have multiple credit cards, I typically suggest the "debt snowball plan," which has you pay off the smallest balance first, then apply the payment you were making on that credit card to your next lowest balance. With this method, you will probably pay more in interest, but the psychology behind getting rid of card by card is freeing. It can also motivate you to keep going and get rid of that debt for good.

In some cases, you may want to pay down the credit card with the highest interest rate first. This method is called the "debt avalanche plan." Your choice of plan depends on the balances, the interest rates, and your self-discipline to make the necessary changes happen.

## OTHER TYPES OF DEBT

Okay, enough with the credit card debt. I apologize if I caused you stress regarding your own credit card debt. That wasn't my intention, but I really want you to know how bad such debt is for your overall financial

---

10   Undebt.it is a free online debt snowball calculator and management tool that will help you quickly develop a debt elimination payment plan. "The Free Tool That Gets You Out of Debt," Undebt.it, accessed July 2022, https://undebt.it/.

well-being. I want you to live in financial freedom and the way to make that happen is to maintain $0 credit card debt.

Let's move on to other types of debt. Since we already talked a bit about automobile debt, let's discuss that further. Like I said earlier, auto debt is not good debt because your car is a depreciating asset. Most houses hold their value. They can even appreciate. Cars (also trucks, RVs, and boats)—not so much. They usually lose value substantially every year. Ideally, pay cash for your car (unless, as previously stated, your cash becomes an investment and your investment interest is higher than the interest on the car loan). I can hear you responding, "Yeah right, who pays cash? Everybody I know has a car payment. They don't leverage their investments." Though I certainly have witnessed many clients take advantage of this interest rate leverage strategy, it is true that there is no guarantee of gain. Therefore, I agree that paying cash for a car is definitely not the norm. I said, "ideally," didn't I?

Just admit that losing value on your car in conjunction with paying interest on an auto loan doesn't make for the wisest financial decision. Then, with that said I'll add that many people just do not have a choice. They need a car. They cannot pay for it outright. Research your transportation choices to:

- take out a loan (low interest rate only—under 3 percent in today's environment),

- lease a car,

- use ride-share,

- use public transportation,

- carpool.

To minimize depreciation, research when to trade in your car while it still has trade-in value. Whatever you decide, vehicle costs will either show up in your "debt bucket" or your "household expense bucket." It really doesn't matter which. Just make sure that you can afford the expense of a car and that you realize that debt on a car may pull you away from spending on the things that matter most—your core values. If owning and paying for a vehicle are in alignment with your values, then the extra cost is worth it.

I have seen the pain of debt among my clients. Sometimes their situations are heartbreaking. Please avoid such stress whenever possible. Consider the consequences of expenditures in the short run and the long run. Whenever possible, consider refinancing or negotiating to get a lower interest rate and a lower payoff. If you have student loans, private loans, credit cards, auto debt, pay those all off as soon as possible. Don't let your debt control you; you control it!

Once you have a plan for paying down debt, refocus your behavior toward the goal of not getting into any more debt. Make most of your spending intentional, not frivolous or impulsive. Prioritize your spending. Discount sales aren't necessarily a savings after all, especially if you didn't want/need the item all that much to begin with. Happy hours and dinners will cause your wallet to have unhappy hours—days, even years. Save the calories—and the cash.

Know exactly what you are getting for your money and have a plan for paying for it. Prioritize your spending. This may necessitate hiring a financial advisor to keep you accountable for the plan you have formulated together. Accountability to someone is often key to changing past attitudes and behaviors.

**Live for today; save for tomorrow.**
**Prioritize gratification; minimize your debts.**

# Grow Your Financial Wealth and Your Life

**You are ready to implement change because:**
**You have owned it!**

✓ Your beliefs are clarified.

✓ Your values are prioritized.

✓ Your strengths have been highlighted.

✓ Your emotions have been acknowledged.

✓ Your rational mind is in charge.

✓ Your goals, small and large, short- and long-term, have been written.

✓ Your interfering baggage has been shed.

**You are ready to implement change because:
You have earned it!**

✓ Your chosen career has been identified and pursued.

✓ Your present career has been analyzed in terms of your values, goals, and strengths.

✓ Your personalized spending plan has been created.

✓ Your present debt has been laid out in facts and figures.

✓ Your plan for managing your debt has been established.


You have done the work! You are ready to move on. You are ready to grow it! What does "grow it" mean? I am going to share a secret with you that my wealthiest clients know—no one becomes wealthy by just earning an income. It's what you do with that income that unlocks total freedom and increased wealth. Growing your money takes time, education, and attention.

Part three is about growing your financial wealth. As you do so, you secure freedom to spend your time living your life aligned with your values. While I want you to be able to have the money and freedom to live out your values, I also want to share with you how to grow your money to give to your family, to your community, and to our world. I believe this is truly living in abundance.

Many people hold tight to their money because they believe there isn't enough of it or that having more money will guarantee happiness.

Neither is true. First, there is enough money for you if you avoid limiting your thinking and behaviors regarding your earning potential. Second, money will bring you happiness only when it is integrated appropriately into your life and is spent on the things and experiences that you value most.

Before you read any further, I want to offer you some words of encouragement. In a perfect world, what I will be sharing in part three would already be familiar to you, and you would have started to incorporate these principles into your overall financial plan since you first began earning money. However, I've become a realist through years of experience. While working at my first jobs in my twenties, I was only interested in making money and in spending money. Saving, investing, and insuring my money just weren't in my thoughts. Heck, I discovered over a ten-year period that I wasn't even in the right career for me, let alone growing my money wisely.

Many, many "aha" moments occurred as I studied to be a financial advisor. Not only did I learn how to help clients grow their money, but I also learned how to grow my own. My learning curve was Mt. Everest high. There are numerous financial decisions I *shoulda, woulda, coulda* done differently. Since life often does not give us do-overs, I focused on being grateful for all I was learning. I was most eager to share with my clients any of my knowledge in order to benefit them. I still have most of my clients from those early years of my practice. I can say with confidence that I took them from wherever they were and that the vast majority of them significantly grew their wealth and worth as we worked together over the years.

So, as you read through the following content, please don't focus on the past except to learn from it. Regrets waste your time and energy. You are where you are now. Read. Learn. Consider the "ideal." Then, modify that "ideal" to fit your unique situation, but move forward.

Change what you can now. Commend yourself for your willingness to become educated and to create new plans, to set and work toward new goals. Commit to making the very most of what you have learned and earned.

## CHAPTER 9

# Taking Action with a Plan for Saving

In this chapter, I want you to see the "big picture" first. I want to give you an overview of the components that go into creating your comprehensive wealth alignment plan. I'd like you to review saving, insuring, investing, and dealing with taxes. You can find detailed information in books and in online resources such as courses, forums, and YouTube videos. However, this section was drawn from my realistic approach to these topics after advising clients one-on-one for over two decades.

I think back to my pre-advising days when much of what is in this chapter was a language I didn't understand or frankly, even care about. Now, I wish I had known more sooner. My goal is to give you some basic information, enough that you can do research or ask questions for further information about any facet that is pertinent to you and your financial planning.

The various components of a comprehensive wealth alignment plan are found listed on the worksheet below. As you "check it out" on the pages that follow, you will be given further details for each topic. Whenever you choose to act on any of these, you can then "check it off."

## Grow Your Financial Wealth

**Check It Out**                                          **Check It Off**

- Fill Buckets of Savings

  – Bucket #1: Cash Reserves                          _____

  – Bucket #2: Short- and
    Mid-Term Expenditures                             _____

  – Bucket #3: Long-Term Expenditures

  – Financial Independence                            _____

  – Retirement                                        _____

- Insure Your Wealth

  – Health/Medical Insurance                          _____

  – Disability Insurance                              _____

  – Life Insurance                                    _____

  – Other Insurances

  – _____                        _____

  – _____                        _____

  – _____                        _____

- Invest Your Money

  – Decide Time and Purpose                           _____

  – Short-Term Investment                             _____

- – Long-Term Investment  $\rule{2cm}{0.4pt}$
- – Diversify  $\rule{2cm}{0.4pt}$
- • Get Help from an Expert
- – Broker  $\rule{2cm}{0.4pt}$
- – A Registered Investment Advisor  $\rule{2cm}{0.4pt}$
- – A Robo-Advisor Platform  $\rule{2cm}{0.4pt}$
- • Take Care of Taxes
- – Taxable, Non-qualified Accounts  $\rule{2cm}{0.4pt}$
- – Tax-Deferred, Qualified Accounts  $\rule{2cm}{0.4pt}$
- – Tax-Free, Qualified Accounts  $\rule{2cm}{0.4pt}$
- • Avoid Distractions  $\rule{2cm}{0.4pt}$

## THE IMPORTANCE OF SAVINGS

I cannot stress enough how important it is to save. The first step (after earning your income) is learning how to "pay yourself" first through the act of saving. Most Americans are struggling to save enough for their futures, including retirement.

Remember in the "Earn It" section, how we created your spending plan? This was designed to make sure that all your expenditures were in alignment with the values and goals you had established. Likewise, now you need a savings plan, one that has been knowledgeably formulated and tailored to your specific income and goals. Developing a savings plan is essential to making the most of your money, to protect what you earn while also growing your wealth.

Feeling secure is one of our basic human needs. If our spending behavior isn't resulting in security, then we need to make simple but impactful changes. We need to become more effective in managing our money. We need to learn how to save.

**Saving a portion of your income enables you to live a life of security and freedom.**

What is your right amount to save? As you have learned in the "Earn It" section of this book, I, as a CFP®, urge my clients to commit to saving a minimum of 15 percent of their gross incomes, because this amount of savings will allow them to grow their wealth. Fifteen percent? Seems like a lot, I'm guessing. I'm imagining your raised eyebrows! Yes, you can; you can afford to save this amount. You work extremely hard to earn your money and in turn you need to have that money work equally hard for you.

It is almost impossible to become WELLthy™ (meaning living in total alignment with yourself and your wealth) from income alone. Only by saving a portion of your income will you be able to live a life of security and freedom. This, of course, assumes you are not inheriting any wealth. And, even if it's probable that you will receive an inheritance, you certainly want to be able to increase your personal and financial worth with that money, not have to use it only to pay off debt. I cannot stress enough how important it is to save and grow a portion of your money.

There are two tactics that work together, I believe, to guarantee saving success:

1. Make use of compound interest. Earning interest on your saved money allows your money to grow over time. Each time interest is applied, it is to a larger total, resulting in an even larger total.

2. Put your savings on autopilot! Yep, it's that simple. Automate your savings. A specific amount of money is taken out of every paycheck, every time, and put into a separate account(s). Out of sight, out of mind.

## DAWN'S STORY—AUTOMATING SAVINGS

Some of my very first clients, a young couple, came to me with the following goals:

- "We want to build our first home in a safe, comfortable neighborhood;
- "We want to have a third child;
- "We want to provide our children with more experiences than we had growing up; and
- "We want to live guilt-free and not be envious or jealous of our friends' lifestyles."

They had a total household income of approximately $75,000. They also had $8,000 in credit card debt, no cash reserves built up, and no income or life protection. I believed they were overpaying their annual tax bill. Their 401ks were worth $18,000.

Now, twenty-one years later, they remain clients of mine. They have an investment net worth of over $3,000,000. I recently asked them what they would tell their children who are now beginning their own financial journeys. They said the secret to their success was twofold: one, they committed early on to their goals, including savings, with clarity and certainty that they would achieve them; and two, they had me along as an advice/accountability partner. They added that they never felt like they had to sacrifice their chosen lifestyle. This was because their commitment to savings occurred even before any of their money landed in their checking account. They automated savings. They followed my two nonnegotiable rules. First, pay taxes. Second, save at least 15 percent of your gross income and live on the rest.

## SAVE "BUCKETS" OF MONEY

When saving money, I suggest that you compartmentalize your money as follows:

- Savings Bucket #1—Build Power Cash Reserves

    The first savings bucket is for cash reserves, what I call "power cash." Requiring yourself to maintain cash reserves is the first critical step in growing your financial worth. Commit 5 percent (of the recommended 15 percent savings amount) to this bucket. Power cash provides financial security in times of crisis. It puts you in control and gives you power. It goes a long way toward preventing financial distress or disaster. When people are caught not having enough cash on hand, there is no financial "security" that allows them to support sound decision-making for their families or careers in times of unplanned change.

    Sometime in our adult lives most of us will face some kind of crisis. This could involve health issues of self or family, loss of a job, economic downturn, natural disasters, or a pandemic. In my opinion, having power cash on hand is a nonnegotiable aspect of sound financial planning. I know life is expensive, and many of us, including me, would like to spend everything we make. We work extremely hard for our pay, and we want to enjoy the rewards of earning. Because we live in an immediate gratification society, it is dangerously easy to be influenced to "get it now." However, what we want to do and what would be wise to do are two different things. We must find the balance between spending and saving.

I understand and empathize with you as you contemplate this task. Building up cash in a savings or money market account can feel boring and unfulfilling. We want that dinner out or those trendy handbags now because we either had an insane week or we worked way too many hours and we deserve these things. Right? Yes, we do. Honestly, you probably deserve more! You deserve to live in financial freedom and security. You need to get yourself to where you can buy more than dinner or the handbag—but only once your power cash reserve is built up. Financial freedom comes from initial sacrifice. This sacrifice doesn't take long, but it is imperative that you delay gratification early on for your journey to financial wealth. This is the short-term pain for long-term gain I discussed early in this book.

I'm guessing that you or you and your spouse could come up with any number of ways to cut expenditures for things or activities you really wouldn't miss all that much, but that would give you money to add to your savings. Yes, you may decide to reduce or eliminate a few fun purchases or activities. However, do you know what is really fun? It is watching your power cash fund grow. It's knowing you are in control of your spending decisions. When you know you could spend more, but you choose not to, that is empowering and enriching!

The ultimate goal is to build three to six months of your monthly living expenses for a cash reserve. I admit saving this amount can be overwhelming, so your initial plan may be to get your power cash reserves up to a balance of $2,000, which would be an ideal place to start.

Once you've achieved your $2,000, you will then realize that reaching this balance was easier than you expected. Next, you can reset your power cash reserves goal until you reach that three- to six-month recommendation.

I suggest this money be saved in a money market account at a brokerage firm, not at the bank where you have your checking account. That way you will not be tempted to transfer money back and forth from checking to savings when your checking account balance is low. Once you have met your cash reserve goal, then go ahead and transfer it back to your bank savings account. By this time, it is safe to have the cash at your bank; you have already demonstrated the self-control you needed to create the security of a cash reserve. Now you'll have access if money is needed for a crisis. I promise you will never regret the financial discipline that built up your cash reserve. On the other hand, I believe you will regret that dinner, handbag, and other purchases that sabotaged your real power, the power of self and the power of wealth.

## DAWN'S STORY—CASH FOR LIFE'S CURVEBALLS

My clients, a married couple with two young children, did not have any "power cash." Their "in case of emergency" plan was to use credit cards. Each time I saw them, I promoted the advantages of establishing cash reserves.

Two years into our planning relationship, their incomes grew by 30 percent, and so did their expenses. One day they pulled up to my office for their financial planning meeting in their brand-new truck that cost them $750 per month.

About four months later, one of life's curveballs hit them. The breadwinner of this family was laid off from work for nine months. Not only were they suffering from the lack of income, but their expenses escalated due to unforeseen medical bills. In no time they were strapped with debt but had no cash reserves. Within three months, they sold their home at a loss and the family squeezed into a tiny apartment. That $750/month truck was repossessed and their credit rating tanked. It was their spending decisions, one after another, that mushroomed into disaster. A three- to six-month bucket of cash reserves would have saved them their home, their truck, their dignity, and their security. Their situation made me sad and I felt helpless as their wealth advisor.

- Savings Bucket #2—Save for Short- and Mid-Term Goals

To me, a short- or mid-term goal is set for a major expenditure(s) you plan to make in the next three to seven years. That may be money for a down payment on a house, a new car, a vacation, or to celebrate a special event. There are multiple factors to consider when formulating a savings plan to fill this bucket. One of them is the years available for saving. Others are the rate of returns and fees on investments. I will say unequivocally, saving earlier is the key to faster financial success.

Be cautious when you are investing for your short-term goals. The shorter the time horizon you have to achieve your goal, the less risk you should be taking on with your investments. Risk and your time horizon go hand in hand. The less time you have to achieve your goals, the less risk you should take, and the more time you have to achieve your goals, the more risk you should consider taking.

- Savings Bucket #3—Save for Long-Term Goals

Long-term goals are for "down-the-road," larger expenses such as buying a larger home, another car, a "dream" vacation, or sending a child off to college. Of course, long term also includes saving for retirement. As with saving for short-term goals, there are multiple factors to consider when formulating a savings plan to fill this bucket. One of them is the years available for saving. Others are the rate of returns and fees on investments. Again, I will say unequivocally, saving earlier is the key to faster financial success. For the most part, in planning for their retirement, I urge my clients to aim for the following:

A Rule of Thumb: Have an investment portfolio of fifteen times your last pre-retirement gross annual income.

Milestones to Consider Achieving:

- Having saved the equivalent of your current annual salary by age 30.

- Having saved three times your current annual salary by age 40.

- Having saved six times your current annual salary by age 50.

- Having saved eight times your current annual salary by age 60.

- Having saved ten times your current annual salary by age 67.

You get the idea. Please note that the later a person begins saving, the more that person must save each year in order to meet the suggested goal of saving fifteen times one's current gross income. The longer you wait, the older you are and the less time you have to save. As the years pass by, even though you will have reached a higher income level, you'll still need to save even more to give yourself financial security by the time you are retired. No one wants that. I again want to emphasize that what gets people into financial trouble is waiting too long to start saving. However, just an encouraging reminder, better to save late than never!

## KICK-START YOUR SAVINGS PLAN

Here is a list of strategies you can implement immediately to help minimize some of your current non-core value expenses and apply this freed-up money to kick-start your savings plan:

- Restructure debt. Take all your high interest, non-tax write-off debt like your auto loans, credit card payments, medical debt, and even your student loans and negotiate the interest on those balances. You can even hire a debt consolidation company (or even your existing bank) to negotiate on your behalf and get your payments down to one manageable payment.

- Review all lines of your insurance payments. If you haven't done a competitive analysis with your homeowners, auto, umbrella, and health/medical insurances within the last twelve to eighteen months, you could be overpaying for your protection.

- Minimize your tax bill. I urge you to consult a tax specialist for assistance in minimizing your tax burden.

## PROTECT YOUR WEALTH ALIGNMENT PLAN WITH INSURANCE

Though I believe people understand the value of insurance, I have found that most of those I have worked with are underinsured and/or have the wrong type of insurance in place. Without enough insurance, hard-earned income and savings could be lost in the blink of an eye when life throws us those curveballs.

Unexpected medical bills, illness, injury, layoffs, premature death, natural or financial disasters are risks we all live with. Most of us don't much like talking about these realities, but we cannot afford to live with the mentality of "it won't happen to me."

Protection planning is extremely important in creating security and peace of mind. Revisiting the cost for these benefits is completely worth the effort and should be done on a regular basis. No wealth alignment plan is secure (or even matters) until we have protection in place!

There are so many types of insurance, and advising on any of them requires knowledge of an individual's circumstances. So as not to have you drown in detail, I will list a few types of insurance, some key points for each, and then strongly urge that you seek expertise in these areas.

### Health/Medical Insurance

- Plans vary greatly; they need to be fully explained by the people providing/selling them.
- You need to do plenty of comparing of the information you

are given from various sources. If you need assistance, consider connecting with a fiduciary wealth advisor to give you unbiased advice on the best type of plan to implement.

- You want facts and figures on coverage of various expenses; some plans are comprehensive, others are not.

- There is public health insurance and private health insurance, which may be provided by an employer or can be purchased at the marketplace.

- Some type of health/medical insurance coverage is extremely important to protect yourself and your family.

## Disability Insurance

Here are some sobering statistics that point to the need to take disability seriously:

- According to Social Security Disability Statistics, a "sobering fact for twenty-year-olds is that more than one in four of them becomes disabled before reaching retirement age."[11]

- "About 30 percent of Americans ages 35-65 will suffer a disability lasting at least ninety days during their working careers."[12] That's one out of three people. Scary.

- "About one in seven people ages 35-65 can expect to become disabled for five years or longer."[13]

---

11  "Facts," U.S. Social Security Administration (website), accessed July 2022, https://www.ssa.gov/disabilityfacts/facts.html.

12  "Disability Statistics and Facts," Affordable Insurance Protection (website), accessed July 2022, https://www.affordableinsuranceprotection.com/disability_facts#:~:text=About%2030%20percent%20of%20Americans.

13  "What are my chances?," Affordable Insurance Protection (website), accessed July 2022, https://www.affordableinsuranceprotection.com/odds_of_disability.

And, because of these statistics, disability insurance is important because:

1. First, it involves protecting your most valuable asset, your ability to earn an income.

2. Second, without an income, your wealth planning won't work.

Therefore, my suggestions regarding disability insurance are to:

- Take advantage of any disability insurance offers from your employer as soon as you are hired.

- Check out offerings of short-term (zero to six months) and long-term insurance (six months plus).

- Weigh the pros and cons of the premium cost of each type. Long-term insurance costs tend to be more expensive than short-term.

- Assess what's best for you. If you haven't achieved your cash reserve goal to compensate for any loss of short-term income, you definitely need short-term income protection. If you have cash reserves in place, consider long-term disability coverage. Check to see if short-term coverage is included in your employer-sponsored plan at no additional cost. However, I believe that even if it is, you still need your power cash reserves for other emergencies.

- Implement both the employer and supplemental disability coverage. This would be ideal.

- Rarely have I found any of my clients excited to discuss disability insurance, let alone implement a disability plan. I understood how important this protection was, but many clients thought they would never get sick or injured, so I had a hard time implementing this protection for them. I realized how important it was and needed to address their risk from a broader perspective. I showed clients that in the event they became disabled, their ability to achieve their goals decreased to almost 0 percent. The cost of this protection was minimal based on a risk versus return perspective.

- I remember spending significant time discussing disability insurance with one of my clients who was a flight attendant. I told her if she became disabled, she wouldn't be able to fly and she would lose a significant amount of income. The loss of income would result in her not being able to fund her kids' education or retire.

- This client who implemented my advice and her disability plan ended up with leukemia. Her disability plan has paid her for more than ten years, and not once were either she or her husband stressed about their finances. Instead, they could focus on getting her healthy and enjoying the time they had together. A small insurance premium to pay for the peace of mind. Unfortunately, this client is currently in hospice and called me last week to tell me how grateful she was for this advice. I told her how grateful I was to be able to serve her family.

**Protect your most valuable asset—your ability to earn an income.**

## Life Insurance

- Life insurance may not be necessary for individuals who:
    - Are without family and are depending on their income and/or assets for survival.
    - Have already become financially independent.
- Life insurance is very necessary for most individuals:

- In the event of a premature death where family members are relying on the deceased's income and savings.

- For estate planning purposes where minimizing estate taxes is a primary goal.

• The amount and type of life insurance to get varies:

  - To fully figure out the exact amount you need, it is necessary to have a serious conversation with a spouse or significant other about the amount of money necessary for the survivor's lifestyle to continue.

  - I have learned that many people need the equivalent of five times their gross income plus the total amount of their outstanding debt.

  - To ascertain the correct amount for you as an individual, couple, or family may require professional expertise.

  - An expert can also help you determine what type of insurance to implement, for example, term insurance, permanent insurance, or a combination of the two. The premiums you must pay for term insurance are usually the most cost-effective way to meet your overall needs.

  - Insurance is expensive. Term insurance is the least expensive type of life insurance. Spending minimal money on a term policy assures that if you were to pass away prematurely, your family is covered.

  - Permanent insurance is more expensive but also includes an investment component. That is, you would be allowed to add money to your premium, thus using it as an investment vehicle. After a period of time, typically ten to fifteen years, you will be able to pull out money tax-free from the policy to spend however you choose, as long as the insurance policy stays in force.

## Other Types of Insurance, Including but Not Limited to:

- dental and vision insurance

- long-term care insurance

- homeowners insurance

- auto and other vehicle insurance

- umbrella insurance (This is liability insurance that is in excess of that specified in other policies. Potentially this insurance could be the primary insurance for losses not covered by other policies.)

- pet insurance

## INVEST YOUR MONEY

Make sure you have embraced the concept that saving money is a non-negotiable item within your overall financial plan. Recall that investing is one way to make the most of saving money. Investments grow, and interest compounds over time. There are many options for investments, including stocks, bonds, mutual funds, exchange-traded funds, real estate, commodities, hedge funds, alternative investments, and cryptocurrency, to name a few.

Determine the best places to secure your savings—that 15 percent of your gross income you've set aside.

## Short- and Mid-Term Goals

For pursuing short- and mid-term goals in three to seven years (vacations, down payment on a house, purchasing a car, holiday savings), look for non-qualified investments or savings accounts (those not qualified for any special tax treatments, such as IRAs).

Your earnings will be either taxable on an annual basis and/or when you sell that investment at capital gains rates, which are often less than ordinary income tax rates. An advantage to an ordinary investment or savings account is you have access to this account at any time.

## Long-Term Goals

If you're pursuing a time frame greater than seven years, such as retirement, look for qualified accounts, those allowing special tax treatment (tax-deferred or tax-free).

Your money will grow more efficiently due to the simple fact that instead of this money being taxed annually, it stays invested and will compound.

These are usually retirement accounts such as traditional and Roth 401k, 403b, PERA 457 plans, traditional IRA, Roth IRA, Simple IRA, or Simplified Employee Pension (SEP). All these plans have requirements to meet based on either employer rules and/or IRS rules.

You either make a Roth retirement plan or Roth IRA with after-tax dollars and pay no tax on the withdrawal. Or, with traditional retirement accounts, pay tax on the entire balance when you withdraw (typically at age fifty-nine and a half), thus your investments should grow at a faster pace. These contributions or withdrawals are taxed at ordinary income rates.

Some important advice about retirement accounts:

- Take advantage of your company's retirement benefit as soon as you are hired at your first job.

- Look at your company's plan. In many cases, if you invest a certain percentage of your income in an employee-sponsored retirement plan, your employer will match that percentage. This is like getting free money!

- Consult with your human resources department or read your employee handbook and/or plan summary descriptions to understand if, when, and how your company contributes to your retirement plan. Also, it's never too early to meet with a wealth advisor who specializes in comprehensive planning to help you determine how much you can afford to save, how much is needed for your future retirement, whether you should do a Roth or traditional plan, and how to minimize your taxes as you save.

If you are looking for non-biased advice, connect with my team and me here: https://dawndahlby.com/own-it-earn-it-grow-it/.

## Diversify Your Investments

Build security to experience future financial freedom. Diversify your investments:

- To get the appropriate mix of different types of investments to help mitigate risk

- To take on the right kind of risk based on your goals, risk tolerance, and time frame

- To find your best "investment mix" of stocks, bonds, real estate, commodities, etc.

- To get the best net dollar benefit possible by minimizing the taxation on your investments

## Find Expert Help

I will list a few different types of professionals you can hire to give you investment and/or comprehensive financial advice. Unless you want to make investing your full-time job, I believe it is imperative that you have a trusted partner you can rely upon for expertise.

- **Broker**: A broker is an agent who does not have the title to an asset but buys and sells for the owner on a commission basis. The relationship with their customers tends to be transaction oriented. Brokers earn commissions from selling stocks, bonds, mutual funds, and other investment products. (A commission is a sum or percentage of what has been paid that is allowed to agents for their services.) Brokers can only recommend investments that they reasonably believe are appropriate for the given situation, but they are not required to offer the lowest-cost investments.

- **Independent Registered Investment Advisor (RIA)**: RIAs are regulated by the Securities and Exchange Commission (SEC), a government agency. They are licensed to give advice. Because fee-only advisors are not paid on commission, they usually charge clearly delineated fees for the advice and management services they provide. A fee-only or fee-based fiduciary advisor is legally responsible for choosing suitable investment solutions that are also the most cost-effective.

- **Robo-Advisor**: This is a digital, lower-cost alternative for investors who don't have complex needs.

Choosing a broker or advisor is about more than costs, though those can vary greatly. I hope you'll consider how much and what type of advice you need and what type of working relationship you prefer. I'm pretty sure you will want to work with someone you can fully trust to develop the right planning strategy for you, one that includes performance, proper tax allocation, and sound decision-making. Hiring the right type of professional for your financial needs is important. Your goal should be to receive more value from the advice you are receiving than what you are paying.

"Research suggests that people who work with a financial advisor feel more at ease about their finances and could end up with about 15 percent more money to spend in retirement. Additionally, 79 percent of those who use a financial advisor report feeling confident in achieving their retirement goals."[14] Further, "a Vanguard study found that, on average, a hypothetical $500K investment would grow to over $3.4 million under the care of an advisor over twenty-five years, whereas the expected value from self-management would be $1.69 million, or 50 percent less. In other words, an advisor-managed portfolio would average 8 percent annualized growth over a twenty-five-year period, compared to 5 percent from a self-managed portfolio."[15]

As I wrap up this investment section, let me say the best investment you can make is investing in yourself first. Own who you are meant to be and live out your life according to your values. As you invest in yourself, you will also want and need to invest in your future. Like I stated earlier, you cannot become wealthy on your income alone, so turn that income into building real wealth that will support your values

---

14  "Planning & Progress Study 2020," Northwestern Mutual (website), accessed July 2022, https://news. northwesternmutual.com/planning-and-progress-2020.

15  SmartAsset Staff, "7 Mistakes People Make When Choosing a Financial Advisor," *Yahoo! Finance*, March 14, 2022, https://finance.yahoo.com/news/7-mistakes-people-choosing-financial-191657428.html.

and goals throughout your entire life. Nothing creates more peace of mind than knowing you have the money to live in abundance.

## TAKE CARE OF TAXES

Taxes will likely be one of your largest living expenses. Your financial decisions regarding taxes can significantly (positively or negatively) impact your bottom financial line. Just to be clear, my goal is certainly not to educate you on the tax system. You would fall fast asleep in minutes! However, I just have to say that I love discussing taxes because knowing the rules can make a huge positive impact toward living out your values and goals. My goal IS to show you how to live wealthy by minimizing your taxes, thus giving you more money toward your goals.

### Minimize taxes to maximize wealth!

It is important to have a tax balance with both your income and your investments. Tax balance is a combination of managing tax dollars today while simultaneously managing tax dollars for the future. The goal is to minimize your lifelong tax bracket. This means you want to keep your income taxed at similar rates throughout your life. You don't want some years of higher taxation and some years without taxation. You want balance! The goal is to pay minimal taxes every year.

So, how do we get this tax balance? Just like we need diversification in our investments, we need tax diversification in our financial plan. We can diversify as follows:

- **Non-qualified accounts** such as your savings account and your brokerage account

- Money is invested with after-tax dollars, meaning after you have paid federal and state income tax.

- I recommend aiming for 30 percent of your total investable net worth be placed in taxable accounts.

• **Qualified traditional accounts** including your employer-sponsored retirement plans such as 401(k)s, 403(b)s, government plans, and IRAs

  - These accounts are qualified for special tax treatment.

  - Your money is invested into these accounts prior to federal or state taxation.

  - When money is pulled out from these accounts to be used as income, they are taxed at ordinary income rates. The benefit of putting money away that hasn't been taxed is that you have the opportunity to invest more money up front. The money grows tax-deferred. However, when you pull money out, typically in retirement, it's 100 percent taxable.

  - I recommend 40 percent of your total investable net worth be placed in tax-deferred accounts.

• **Tax-free qualified accounts** such as Roth IRAs, municipal bonds, and some permanent life insurance products

  - This money is invested with after-tax dollars.

  - It usually grows tax-free.

  - When the money is pulled out, typically in retirement, there will be no taxes due.

  - I recommend 30 percent of your total investable net worth be placed in tax-free accounts.

These recommendations are designed to give you the opportunity to save tax dollars today as well as in the future. However, in financial planning, everyone's needs and circumstances are different and require a customized approach for maximum benefit. You need to search out a tax expert you trust to deliver advice tailored to your situation.

The goal is to plan and to save more than just a few tax dollars. When you plan well, you save well, which allows you to spend well, too! That is the name of the game—how one builds and lives with real wealth.

## AVOID DISTRACTIONS

This chapter has focused on growing your wealth. Building cash reserves, saving, protecting your worth through insurance, investing wisely, and knowledgeably dealing with taxes will all allow you to build wealth. I encourage you to pursue all these goal-oriented actions. I also caution you to avoid distractions that could so easily and quickly pull you away from these actions and your goals.

Distractions can come in so many forms. You can easily be influenced by family and friends who do not share your values or your discipline. Invitations to go out for over-priced dinners or join in on a luxury cruise can sabotage your long-term goals. That easily accessible Amazon app lies in wait for you to click "Buy Now." Doubt easily attacks suggestions that you put out money monthly or annually for insurances "I may never need." Past spending habits can so quickly lure you back. Credit cards entice you toward impulsive spending and increased debt.

Life's responsibilities, lack of commitment and support from a significant other, and any number of fears can tear you away from what you have already thoughtfully and purposely established as changes you need and want to make in your life. Having an expert who knows you and your portfolio, and who you trust, will help encourage you while also holding you accountable to your stated techniques and goals. That advisor can help you regain confidence and reestablish your values.

Stick to your goals. Carry out your plan for achieving those goals. Do this for you. Your worth and wealth are at stake here! If you do have a significant other with whom to share this undertaking, you two have found a true bonding in sharing values and goals and thus creating financial freedom and security together.

As you pursue growing your wealth, it is essential to remind yourself that the two biggest commodities in the lives of earning adults are time and money. We've learned that most adults spend approximately 40 percent of their waking hours working in their chosen career. We now know that using your unique strengths while working that career can certainly maximize your time use as well as your income potential.

You have also learned that it is ideal to spend 25 percent of my version of net income according to your five core values. Let the magic begin as you live out what is most important to you. Experience internal security as you own yourself. Saving, investing, and protecting your money can add greatly to your external security as you earn it. A complete financial plan, created with an advisor working in your best interests, will help you avoid life's distractions while you earn through your strengths and spend around your values. These are the keys to a security and freedom you will cherish.

Finally, I want to commend you sincerely and proudly for wading through complex topics in this chapter. I believe as you pursue further information and get answers to additional questions you may have, you'll be better able to systematically work toward your goal of a comprehensive wealth management plan.

# CHAPTER 10

# Leaving a Legacy

I truly believe that most people desire a life filled with happiness and joy. What brings them such feelings will vary widely. Loving and being loved, living one's faith, interacting with family and friends, reveling in nature, and achieving success can all lead to exclamations of "That made me so happy." I propose that two less-voiced aspects of life that also lead to pure joy and happiness are growing and giving.

Growing implies change in a positive direction. Those committed to personal growth have put in the time to learn about themselves, their values, and their worth. They have read multiple personal development books and perhaps sought out counselors or life coaches. In turn they have made behavioral adjustments in their lives that reflect their beliefs and values. They are intent on walking their talk. They have become a better version of themselves. They are effective communicators, okay with recognizing their weaknesses, and humble when acknowledging their strengths and efforts. They are secure enough to apologize, to compromise, to learn and teach, and to ask for help when needed. They are comfortable in their own skin. They are to be admired. Their journey has certainly been challenging. They are living internal personal wealth.

So far you have worked to further your growth as a whole person while also growing your money. Owning the entirety of who you are and believing that the capacity for making changes is always available to you allows you to feel security within, plus a confidence and capability to deal with whatever life throws at you. Learning to grow your money using knowledge, options, and the expertise of others provides financial security as well as a variety of opportunities. You are living external personal wealth.

It has been my experience that when one feels happy, when a person experiences joy, there is a powerful desire to share those emotions with others. "I'm happy; I really want you to be happy, too." From that proclamation springs the spirit of giving. I'm sure you have experienced the genuine pleasure of giving to others, whether it be of your time or your resources.

For me, my greatest fulfillment comes from sharing the rewards of my success with others. Being happy makes me want to give; giving makes me happy. This isn't a vicious circle, it's a victorious circle! This is living internal and external wealth. This is living WELLthy™!

## DAWN'S STORY—THE JOY OF GRATITUDE

Giving to others freely and without a hidden agenda to get something back, I believe, is a by-product of gratitude. I have not always been a thankful person. For years, my natural tendency was to wake up each morning regretting things I did and didn't do the day before. Then I would move on to all that I needed to accomplish on this day. Sometimes by the time I actually got out of bed, I was in a bad mood, overwhelmed, and fearful. Certainly not a good way to start the day. Through reading, praying, and learning from others, I have changed.

I now make it a point to start each day reflecting on three things for which I am most grateful. These might be very simple things like being thankful for the sun shining through my window or much-needed rain watering my flowers or my two small dogs snuggling next to me. They can be the specifics of really big things involving family (a patient husband and two smart daughters), my health (a body that is still fully functioning at fifty), my home (a cleansing, refreshing shower), a career (that challenges and rewards me). I could go on and on. I have made a habit of starting my day with thoughts of gratitude. I am working on bringing thankfulness to mind throughout every day. And honestly, it's been miraculous.

Gratitude for anything and everything has changed my behavior. It puts things into perspective. I try very hard even when things aren't going well to find something in the mess to be grateful for. I remember the day one of my girls was home from school, sick with the flu. I hated seeing her miserable, stumbling from bed to bathroom. I wanted and needed to spend time taking care of her. I did that but with additional anxiety about getting behind in my work. Concern that I would get the flu also permeated my thoughts. In short, she was sick; I was stressed.

And then I caught myself. "Stop. It's the flu. It is not a life-threatening disease. It will pass. If I must, I can catch up on work tonight or this weekend. I need to take care of my girl and myself." And you know what happens the more you practice any skill? You get better at it.

I am trying my hardest to make a habit of positivity and gratitude. And, it's working. It gets easier all the time. I have challenged myself to put a positive spin on everything. Yeah, just so you know, the operative word here is "try." Sometimes I fail and my behavior isn't pretty. But, it is improving. I repeat, I'm a work in progress.

I already know that the more thanks I express, the more mature and responsible my behavior becomes, the more balanced my life feels, and the more I am able and eager to give. I am totally committed to having an attitude of gratitude and expressing my thanksgiving by giving to others.

## NONFINANCIAL GIVING

No matter your checking account or your savings account, you can still give if you wish. Volunteer opportunities are limitless in schools, churches, community organizations, even online sharing of your talents, skills, and wisdom with others. Long- or short-term involvement will be valued. Short visits with lonely and grieving people are deeply appreciated, as are phone calls, greeting cards, emails, and texts. Whenever you help fill someone else's needs in big or small ways, you are making a positive difference.

I often think of the saying "Charity begins at home." When your time and energy are limited, I think giving should start with your very own family. Putting a puzzle together with your fourth grader or actively listening to your high schooler's fears of the future or problems with a boyfriend is time well spent. Giving yourself to your child is a lasting gift. It shows your love of them, and models love for them.

## FINANCIAL GIVING

Like volunteer opportunities, needs for your gifts of money are limitless. Any charity will tell you there is no gift too large or too small. When working with clients on their spending plan, I check out their interest in giving. If that is a desire, I suggest they set aside 5 percent of their income after taxes and savings for charitable giving. This percentage could be given out in various monetary donations or taken into consideration regarding money spent on expenses related to volunteering, spending time with a needy individual, or sending thoughtful cards and gifts.

I believe the act of giving is essential for all of us; how we choose to give is purely an individual decision. I just know our world can use more grateful people and more givers. I believe each of us gains tremendously from giving. I know I have.

## INSPIRING OTHERS

You have been working on growing your total worth, including your self-worth and your net worth. You have come to understand the meaning of the word *wealth* in its broadest, fullest meaning. As a result of working through the content of this book, I believe you not only know yourself better, but you are well on your way to living out your beliefs and values.

I have been going through this process of personal and professional transformation for over twenty years now. I am happier and more secure than I have ever been. I have more financial freedom. Though I certainly do not believe I am finished growing, I have come to the point where I am so fulfilled that I just want to share anything and everything with you that has worked for me. I believe, if you choose to work on defining and realigning yourself, you will be on your way to living WELLthy™. And in the future, you will be able to share with others what has worked for you.

When others observe your joy, confidence, elevated self-esteem, success, gratitude, and your giving, they become curious. They want to know what has changed with you. Explain as you wish. I believe your new path, as mine has, will not only lead to more self-fulfillment and increased wealth but to spreading messages of overall worth through your words and your actions. This has become a goal I am deeply committed to. I want to inspire others to follow in this positive direction, living their beliefs, values, strengths, and goals to the fullest, and in return receiving the very best life has to offer. Who would you like to inspire?

## TEACH YOUR CHILDREN

Who did you decide you'd most like to inspire? If you have them, I truly hope your answer is "my children." In talking with other parents for years, I can't fathom the number of times I have heard "I just want my child to be happy." I heartily agree. If you are a parent, I bet you want the same.

I would expand upon that to say that I want everybody to be happy. Can you imagine what a positive difference it would make in our world if more people were happy?

Realistically, however, I know the starting point in my mission is in my own small part of this world. It starts with my husband and my children. I want so much good for them. First, I want my husband to have the best woman and wife I can be to him. I want my girls to have the best mom I can be. I want these three loves of my life to see me constantly trying to grow toward these ends. I want them to see me apologize when I've screwed up, and I want them to see me hold strong to my advice and values. Everything that I have learned in life that helped to move me forward, I want to share with them. I also want to encourage and respect their growth as individuals and support their search for their best selves. This isn't something our children learn in school. It is my job as a parent to teach them. I want it to be my husband's and my job. Gary and I want our daughters to "own it" and "earn it." (And eventually to "grow it" and get off our payroll!)

I also don't believe children learn enough about finances and money in school, either. I truly believe there should be more curriculum devoted to these practical topics. Until that happens, I choose to make sure my own children receive an education on how money works. Even preschoolers can be taught about earning, saving, and spending via parental modeling and conversation. With each successive year, they can be introduced to circumstances which allow them further practice of these skills. As parents we can't forget that our children's education starts with us. Our children are listening to what we are saying and watching what we are doing, even if we don't think they are. They will model our words and behaviors, so we must be aware of the money messages we are sending them.

My dad told me not so long ago, "You can't expect your eighteen-year-old to be a functioning adult just because he/she walks across the stage at high school graduation. He/she needs years of practice at adulting." We all need that practice, even if we are so-called adults!

My ultimate goal is to teach my children to be resourceful humans. I want to help them learn how to build both their internal personal security and their external financial security. I'm attempting to guide them toward independence, not just allowing them to rely on and inherit my resources. I believe we parents must continually ask ourselves, "What (beliefs, attitudes, behaviors, incentives) are my children inheriting from me?"

## CHAPTER 11

# Accentuate Alignment

I use the word *alignment* frequently. That is because I believe being in alignment is vitally important for growing both a person's worth and wealth simultaneously. The Dictionary.com definition of alignment is "a state of agreement or cooperation among persons, groups, nations, etc., with a common cause or viewpoint." My modified use of alignment refers to being in a state of agreement or cooperation within an individual, centered around a cause, a purpose, a mindset, and a lifestyle. Alignment allows an individual to make the most of who they are as a person and as a professional, a money earner.

Achieving alignment is a lifetime goal. Life brings changes. We change. Realigning (adjusting) these changes will be a forever quest. Your initial reaction might be, "Well, that sounds exhausting!" Hey, sometimes life in general is pretty exhausting. The more all aspects of your life are in alignment, the less stress you'll feel, the less exhausted you will be, the more productive you'll be, the happier you'll be.

There is a Chinese proverb that says, "A journey of a thousand miles begins with a single step." And that is exactly the beginning action for every single person contemplating change. Begin. Take a step. Start in the direction you have determined you want to head. Do it now. Take that step and celebrate that you made it.

I believe you have already made many steps. If you have not only read all these chapters, but also worked your way through the action steps, you have completed many, many more steps. Celebrate!

And keep going. I have a quote on my office wall that says, "Don't look back. You're not going that way." I love it. It reminds me to check for alignment. It pokes me to keep going forward. In turn, I poke you. Keep going. Set your next goal(s). Continue your positive actions toward meeting those goals. Those goals most certainly will lead to successes, and as they do, you'll want more.

## KEEP THE MOMENTUM

You will also build the confidence in your ability to make positive change happen. Sustained motivation will come as you see your personal and financial worth and wealth grow. I absolutely promise you that it can work that way because I did it! Easy? Absolutely not! Back steps and side steps along the way? Definitely. Many of them. Lots of work to get back on track? Yes. Worth every bit of effort? ABSOLUTELY!

You have accomplished so much while reading this book. I applaud you! You have recreated and owned all that is you—your updated beliefs, core values, and strengths. You have made progress toward defining your purpose. You have re-examined how you earn your money to decide if you are in the right career for you. You have explored ways to earn more money or decided that you have more wealth than you realized.

Kudos to you if you have constructed a comprehensive financial plan that incorporates mindful spending based on your core values, plus a commitment to savings and debt reduction. You have explored numerous opportunities for protecting yourself and your family against any circumstances that would interfere with your ability to continue earning an income. You have learned how to grow your money through investments and how to deal wisely with taxes in order to experience more freedom and security in the present, as well as in your retirement years. I'm sure that you have given some thought to the legacy you'd like to leave behind for those you love. Finally, I hope you have concluded, as I have, that alignment of all aspects of our lives is really the key to achieving personal and financial worth and wealth.

## Action Steps—Wrapping up with Pride

I'm laughing even as I write "action steps." I can almost see and hear your reaction: "No, Dawn, please. No more homework!" Not to worry. Remember, we are in celebration mode at this point. Because "alignment" is so key to growing your wealth, I'd like you to write down your achievements in this area. So, as you read each question, brag about what you have accomplished thus far. There is no positive change too small to celebrate.

1. Give evidence that you have aligned your values, beliefs, strengths, and purpose with your personal and financial goals.

———————————————————————————

———————————————————————————

———————————————————————————

———————————————————————————

———————————————————————————

———————————————————————————

———————————————————————————

2. Give evidence that there is alignment between the work that you do to earn money and the goals you have set.

_____

_____

_____

_____

_____

_____

_____

3. Give evidence that you have realigned your spending to reflect the goals you wish to pursue.

_____

_____

_____

_____

_____

_____

4. Give evidence of the various ways in which you are growing your financial wealth.

_____

_____

_____

_____

_____

_____

Way to go! You must feel proud of both your personal and financial growth. Yes, I know, you're not done yet! None of us are. Developing and living the comprehensive wealth alignment plan that we have been discussing is a lifetime endeavor, one that gets easier to execute with each year of our successes. When we see a plan work, we want to keep working it.

Checking on the alignment of all aspects of our wealth building will, hopefully, become a lifelong habit. As you reap the benefits of the persistent practice of "own it," "earn it," and "grow it," you will be motivated to continue pursuing worth and wealth.

**Aligning all aspects of our lives is the key to achieving personal and financial worth and wealth.**

# Conclusion

The demands on each of our lives are so great. I fully appreciate that you took time to read the information I have given you. I am honored.

Many of you may not have had time yet to complete all the action steps. That's okay. Please keep coming back to the book and dip in as many times as needed. It is meant to be your companion on your lifelong journey of discovery and growth. I also hope my personal stories have assured you that I, too, am still learning and growing. The process is always unfolding.

Now that you are aware that these tools are at your disposal, I hope they will inspire you to action and results. My most sincere wish for you is that you will use this book to live authentically in alignment with your wealth and worth. I want you to live with respect for your own personal growth journey and encourage the growth of others, that is, live and give in abundance.

When you earn with your strengths, spend on your values, and save for your goals, you will build personal security and grow financial security—a combination none of us should ever live without.

**Own your worth. Earn your wealth. Grow your life. Live WELLthy™.**

**–DAWN DAHLBY**

# More Designed for You...

- To build your "Own It, Earn It, Grow It" customized plan, visit dawndahlby.com/programs

- Find "The Wealth Factor Alignment Plan" by visiting dawndahlby.com/programs

- For CPA or CFP® services, check out dawndahlby.com/legacy-by-releve

- To find the "Core Values Online Exercise," visit dawndahlby.com/resources

- To find the "What's Your Worth Quiz," visit dawndahlby.com/resources

- For CFP® Institution, search at https://www.cfp.net

- To seek out BFA Certification, visit think2perform.com/our-services/programs/behavioral-financial-advice

# Acknowledgments

Being an author is a multiple-year process going from ideation to publication. There's no way I could have published *Live WELLthy* without the support from too many to mention. If you and I have previously crossed paths, please know I have learned something from you and it's woven into my thought leadership platform designed to lead others to aligned wealth and worth.

I would like to thank my husband Gary, my high school sweetheart, for encouraging me to write this book. We have experienced so much together and I love that we continually work on improving our lives. I could not have built the wealth advisory firm I have today without your continued belief in my abilities and your support in managing our estrogen-filled household. Many times your work in helping raise two daughters goes unnoticed. You never ask for a lot, but you offer unconditional love on a daily basis. I smile in gratitude that, after 35 years of marriage, you still turn down my bed at night. I have learned so much from you and how you empathically connect with our girls. Thank you, Gary, for going on this lifelong journey with me and being the leader of our household!

I would like to thank my daughters Olivia and Sophie for giving me purpose and joy. I love you beyond words. As you embark on your life's journey, my ultimate goal for you is to find your own version of Living WELLthy.

I would also like to acknowledge my late mother and her indirect support in my Live WELLthy mission. Through her pain and suffering, she has taught me that nothing is more important than building one's worth and wealth and nothing more satisfying than living life at the intersection of personal and financial security. Mom, I miss you dearly, and want you to know that I'm carrying out your mission to transform people's lives.

I want to express how grateful I am for my stepmother, Anita, who helped formulate my thoughts and get them organized into this book. I love inspiring and showing people how to build a better life. However, streamlining and connecting those thoughts on paper is not my forte. Engaging in lifelong conversations with you and applying your wisdom to better my own relationships has been a perpetual gift. Anita, your talent in writing this manuscript has been a godsend, and I am beyond grateful to partner with you on such an important topic.

Claudia Boutote, Anita and I are beyond grateful for your leadership in helping us develop *Live WELLthy*. On so many levels, it was an honor to work with you. Your wisdom, knowledge, advice, and integrity speak volumes to your expertise. It's rare to find a mentor that balances truth and love, and it was a gift from above to work with you. I'm looking forward to our next project!

Thank you, Dad, for believing in me from that first moment I asked your opinion on whether I would be a good wealth advisor. Your words of wisdom have been extremely impactful and I would not have gotten to this level without your support. Throughout life, daughters look up to their dads for encouragement. Thank you for encouraging me to be all I can be and for those most important words early on in my career: "I believe in you."

I would like to thank my friend Drew Disher for showing me the opportunity to become a wealth advisor. You are an incredible friend, and I admire the life you have built and respect how you lead others to live out their best lives. I'm honored to have you in my life!

Finally, though I haven't yet met John Horman, I want to thank him for coining "WELLthy." When Anita was having lunch with John, her former colleague, she explained the mission of my book as wanting to help people live healthy and wealthy lives to which John responded, "So you want people to live WELLthy." We agree with John, that pretty much says it all.

# About the Author

**D**awn is a Certified Financial Planner and Wealth Wellness Expert who teaches people how to live WELLthy. With over 20 years of experience, Dawn is the country's first Behavioral Financial Advisor, the founder and president of the multi-million-dollar advisory firm Relevé Financial Group, and the creator of the Live WELLthy™ education and financial planning platform. As a fiduciary with over 20 years of experience providing financial advice, she teaches people to save for tomorrow without having to sacrifice living today. Dawn's proprietary process helps people identify what they want out of life, and she provides proven tools so people can get the money to make it happen. Her unique approach seamlessly merges the most effective teachings of self-help and finance, alleviating financial anxiety by ensuring people have spending freedom today *and* tomorrow.

Dawn's engaging coaching style and results-oriented approach to spending and saving has led her to become a sought-after speaker, a regular contributor to *Worth Magazine,* and a media personality offering expert advice on both broadcast and digital media platforms. Dawn is determined to share what she's learned, empowering other women with the skills and encouragement to recognize the connection between their brains and their bank accounts. She launched a platform called Live WELLthy, which walks individuals who don't have access to a financial planner of Dawn's caliber through the process, merging technology with personalized financial advice to help a broader audience.

Dawn grew up in Wisconsin and after graduating from Holmen High School, she attended The University of Wisconsin–Eau Claire, studying Music Education. After two years in Eau Claire, she quit school and was hired to perform as a singer/dancer on a couple of cruise ships. After her performing stint, she moved to Minnesota and graduated from The University of Minnesota with a Bachelor's of Individual Studies degree. She married Gary Jurkovich, with whom she shares two daughters, Olivia and Sophie, and built her Wealth Advisory Practice in Minnesota. In 2018 their family decided to venture to Scottsdale, Arizona, to embrace a warmer climate and enjoy the desert lifestyle.

## COLLABORATIVE PARTNER, ANITA DAHLBY

Anita Dennler Dahlby was born in San Diego, California but moved to a farm near Elgin, Iowa, at age thirteen. She graduated from high school there and went on to earn a Bachelor's Degree in Elementary Education from the University of Northern Iowa. She completed a Master's Degree in School Counseling from the University of Missouri–St. Louis, where she learned the value of journaling as a coping mechanism for life's challenges. Throughout her thirty-four-year career in education, Anita remained passionate about helping young people. She taught elementary and middle school students then served as a middle school and high school counselor for the remainder of her career. During those years, she was also a wife, mother of two, and stepmother of two, rarely missing any of her kids' activities. She has been blessed with seven grandchildren. After retirement in 2002, Anita and her husband Jerry started "RVing" full time, traveling throughout the country and eventually becoming Snowbirds who first wintered in southern California and now currently in Mesa, Arizona. Anita and Jerry suspended their travels to care for her aging father. A Journey to an End is Anita's "raw and real" journal of the last three years of her father's life that included many crises, painful confrontations, encouraging reprieves, and a closure that can only be attributed to divine intervention. Currently she has teamed up with her stepdaughter, Dawn Dahlby, to write *Live WELLthy*.